BETWEEN PREDATOR & PREY

Forty-Two Years a Government Hunter

MIKE HOGGAN

Between Predator & Prey: Forty-Two Years a Government Hunter
Copyright © 2025 Mike Hoggan

All rights reserved.

First Edition

ISBN: 979-8-218-61881-0

Emerging Ink Solutions
Kara Wilson, Editor
www.emergingink.com

Illustrations by Maureen Hoggan

Without limiting the rights under copyright reserved above, no art of this publication may be reproduced, stored in or introduced into a retrieval system, or transmitted in any form or by any means (electronic, mechanical, photocopying, recording, or otherwise), without the prior written permission of both the copyright owner and the above publisher of this book.

Notice: This book is a memoir. It reflects the author's present recollections of experiences over time. Some events have been compressed and some dialogue has been recreated. The conversations in this book come from the author's recollections and do not represent word-for-word transcripts. The author has retold them in such a way as to elicit the feelings and meanings of what was said. In all instances, the essence of the dialogue is accurate.

The names and details of some individuals have been changed to respect their privacy.

For my loving wife, Maureen.

My rock, my inspiration, my everything.

Without your persistence and unwavering dedication, these stories would have faded into memory, lost and forgotten. This book is as much yours as it is mine.

TABLE OF CONTENTS

Introduction: The Coyote That Changed My Life 1

Chapter 1: Wine for Grandpa 8
Chapter 2: The Crazy Sheepherder 14
Chapter 3: Date Night at the Sheep Camp 24
Chapter 4: A Brand New Life 30
Chapter 5: Buzz in the Sudzz 36
Chapter 6: David the Wilderness Chef 44
Chapter 7: The Hutterites 50
Chapter 8: The Visiting Eye Doctor 58
Chapter 9: A Strange Cup of Tea 66
Chapter 10: Ranchers Vows to Kill Grizzly 70
Chapter 11: Do You Smell Something Dead 80
Chapter 12: The Bawling Bear 86
Chapter 13: A Night with the Chicken Lady 92
Chapter 14: Everything Happens for a Reason 98
Chapter 15: Uh-oh! What do We Do Now? 108
Chapter 16: The Spooky Night Hunt at Heart Butte 114
Chapter 17: The Elusive Ghost of Dupuyer Creek 120
Chapter 18: There One Minute, Gone the Next 126
Chapter 19: Fishing for Bears 134
Chapter 20: Dahlie, My Most Terrifying Experience 142
Chapter 21: A Gaggle of Grizzlies 158
Chapter 22: The Scariest Wolf Calling Experience Ever! 168
Chapter 23: The Killer Wolves of Looking Glass 174
Chapter 24: Lions Stalking the Bed & Breakfast 186
Chapter 25: Devil Bear #666 194
Chapter 26: Tagged for Trouble 198
Chapter 27: Unexplained Mutilations 206
Chapter 28: Jade and the Bears of Dupuyer Creek 220
Chapter 29: Big Mistake at Bear Hollow 232

Conclusion 243
About the Author 247

INTRODUCTION

The Coyote That Changed My Life

"Sometimes, it's not the path you're born to, but the one you stumble upon, that shapes the course of your life."

Mike at age 17, Nevada (1975)

During my high school years in Ely, Nevada, I had no idea what I wanted to do for a living. While growing up, I would often visit some friends at the Mellos Ranch a few miles from my hometown of McGill. The good memories we made there helped set the course. It shaped my life and led me to a career spent outdoors.

Katie, age 4, at trapper camp

My dad worked for the mines, as his ancestors before him. His side of the family came from Montana, where my great-grandfather had been a mining boss near Philipsburg during the 1880s before moving to Nevada after the turn of the century. Although mining was a family tradition, my dad always encouraged me not to follow in his footsteps.

In the spring of 1975, I reached the end of my high school years and was working after school and on weekends for the Duck Creek Ranch in eastern Nevada. Upon arriving at the ranch one afternoon, I found everyone was excited as coyotes had killed a calf earlier that morning. Bill, the government trapper, was on his way to help. This news was interesting, to say the least, as coyotes had always fascinated me. However, the chance to meet a real-life government hunter only added to the excitement.

When Bill arrived, I was in awe. He was a short, stalky man in his mid-twenties, and I knew those coyotes were in trouble. From everything I had heard, trappers like Bill could out-shoot, out-trap, out-track, and out-hunt everyone. Little did I know that day that he would be one of several people who would help chart the course of my life.

Bill led the way to the kill site, where we found the calf three-quarters consumed. Examining the trail of blood on the ground, Bill confirmed coyotes had killed it. He said he would set traps, and a plane would arrive to hunt from the air within the next few days. Oh, how I wanted to spend the rest of that day with him and see how the traps were set. At that very moment, I decided this would be my career. Even though I lacked the skills, I was determined to learn them no matter what.

Bill came to the ranch a couple of times a week. When I wasn't there, he caught a coyote at the kill site, and the plane shot a few more. I wished I didn't have to go to school so I could observe. The killing stopped, but Bill continued his trap line until early summer.

In June, after school was out, I was at the ranch when he arrived and was able to go with him. He showed me how to set a trap and look for tracks and sign. I soaked up the knowledge like a sponge.

"So, what do you plan to do in the fall?" Bill asked me a few days after high school graduation.

"Work at the ranch," I replied.

What he said next would forever change the course of my life.

"Come October, I'm taking my camp to the sheep winter range a hundred miles south of Ely. I stay there five days a week, trapping coyotes around the sheep." Bill eyed me. "I could do with some good company. What do you think? You wanna spend the winter with me?"

This was my chance to learn.

I didn't know it then, but that winter was the start of what was to be a lifelong career. It was there I would learn the trade. I'd meet the other trappers and supervisors, including Mike Laughlin, who would later hire me in Nevada but also whom I would follow to Wyoming and then to Montana.

After meeting the Paris family, who had sheep on the winter range, I worked for them for the next two years, obtaining an education in trapping, sheep, horsemanship, coyotes, and mountain lions.

Conversing with the sheepherders, I learned Spanish, which also contributed to my future life as a government trapper.

One April morning, I realized that nature had a plan in place—not only for my life but for the countless other lives I would later touch along the way.

I owe it all to one coyote and the calf that it killed. I can't help but wonder how different my life would have been if not for them.

Throughout my journey, many people entered my life and helped along the way. There are too many to mention, but you will encounter some of them throughout the book. I am sure my mom and dad worried often. However, they supported me through it all.

I had no intention of writing a book. My wife, Maureen, made this happen. Her endless dedication, tireless typing and editing, and constant encouragement pushed me to complete this book.

Sherm Blom is another who immensely helped with this project. A former government trapper and an author himself, his valuable advice, edits, and support are greatly appreciated.

I also want to thank Dexter Oliver, author of several books and various magazine articles and experienced outdoorsman, whose valuable advice and guidance proved invaluable. Last but not least, my editor, Kara Wilson, who perfected it all. I thank her as well.

I have always been a historian and found it amazing how quickly people forget the past. I have often wondered about historical events that took place where I have worked and traveled. About the people who lived and died where I previously have walked. About the people who celebrated and mourned the tragedies of the land.

I am fortunate to have lived through the perfect time in history between the old and new ways. I am glad to get the opportunity to write down some of my experiences for posterity's sake, to share them with future generations.

It's been nearly fifty years, but it seems like yesterday that I went to work at the Paris Ranch and, from there, Wildlife Services. I can still smell the sagebrush and remember the weathered faces of the hard-working people who entered my life. The helicopter rides and encounters with bears, wolves, and coyotes visit me in my dreams nightly. Some names have been changed, but to the best of my memory, what you are about to read is true.

Thanks to Maureen, this part of history and these stories will not be forgotten.

Mike and Maureen Hoggan

WINE FOR GRANDPA

EST • 1977

WHERE EVERY GLASS TELLS A STORY

CHAPTER 1

Wine for Grandpa

"The best lessons on a ranch come from the land, the labor, and the tales told when the day's work is through."

Time passed slower when I was nineteen. The two years I worked for the Paris Ranch seemed like a decade. The Paris family was of French Basque descent, from a small region on the border between France and Spain, and treated me like one of their own rather than an employee. In hindsight, that period was one of the happiest times of my life.

On the northern end of their large ranch were two families, six miles apart. In 1977, the North Ranch was home to Pete, who ran the cows, his wife Mary Jean, and their two sons, Mickey and David. They were close to my age and became like brothers.

The South Ranch was operated by Pete's brother, Bert, who oversaw the sheep, and his wife, Kathy. Their place was where I spent most of my time. Beltran Paris, whom everyone affectionately called "Grandpa" and who was the father of Bert and Pete, lived on the North ranch and was in his eighties.

He arrived at a young age in the United States from France's Pyrenees Mountains to herd sheep. He was a big man who could outwork people half his years. His hands were massive, perhaps the biggest I'd ever seen. With no formal education, he mastered four languages (Basque, French, Spanish, and English) and, with hard work and sheer determination, put together one of the largest ranches in Nevada. Being a soft-spoken, caring person, everyone thought the world of Grandpa Paris.

The ranch was set at the base of a vast mountain range that stretched north and south. Creeks and springs provided plenty of water for livestock and irrigation. A sagebrush flat ran five miles across a long valley to the next row of hills to the west; the nearest town was seventy-five miles away. It wasn't an easy place to live, but it had been their home for many years.

Throughout the ranch's early years, the herders they employed were mainly Basque. The ranch ran both cattle and sheep. Grandpa took good care of his men and realized an experienced herder not only had more lambs to ship in the fall but had one less thing to worry about, knowing he was doing his job. Some of his employees stayed for years.

Tucked away in an old machine shed at the upper ranch, covered in dust, was an assortment of barrels and a large vat made of oak. Until the 1960s, the ranch made many gallons of wine for the Basque herders, who were allotted a gallon a week. Grapes were imported from California every fall because making enough wine to last the year was a tradition.

Beltran Paris, "Grandpa"

Bert, Pete, and the rest of their families didn't drink wine. Grandpa, on the other hand, would have a tumbler full along with his two daily meals. Unless he ate with us at the South Ranch, where only Kool-Aid was served—which may be the reason he didn't often eat there.

One fall day, while taking provisions to a sheep camp in the mountains east of the ranch, I saw an abundance of elderberries. At supper that night, I asked Bert if he remembered how to make wine. He said, "Sure, it's simple." I told him about the elderberries, and he urged me to bring some home the next time I tended camp.

I picked a sack of elderberries a couple of days later, and our winemaking project began. Bert, Kathy, and I removed as many stems as possible and ran the small berries through a blender.

The thick, dark purple liquid was poured into a two-gallon glass jar, and we added a couple of cups of sugar.

Bert explained, "Now we need to find a spot that's not too hot and not too cold. When it ferments, all the skins, stems, and impurities will float to the top. After skimming off and straining, the wine will be ready."

The jar was left to age on the back porch. A few days later, I examined its contents and noticed mold forming on the top. It was fall and the nights had been cooler than usual. After showing the jar to Bert, he said it wasn't warm enough. He suggested I place the jar near the hot water heater in the kitchen of the old farmhouse. This change did the trick, and soon, we could see small purple spots appear on the hot water heater and floor as our wine fermented away.

Two weeks later, Bert looked at the jar and told me the wine should be done. I had always thought wine-making took longer, sometimes years, but what did I know? Bert and I put the jar on the counter, scraped away all the impurities that had floated to the top, and strained the dark purple liquid into two half-gallon whiskey bottles. Taking two glasses, Bert poured a small amount into each and handed me one. I cautiously sipped; it was terrible, with a sharp, sour taste that reminded me of diesel fuel.

After taking a drink, Bert said, "That's not bad; it tastes like a Zinfandel." I didn't know what a Zinfandel was, but I knew right then it was something I would definitely avoid in the future.

The wine went into the refrigerator and aged another week until the day Grandpa arrived for lunch. As we prepared to eat, I asked him if he would like a glass of wine with his meal.

"What? You have wine here?" he asked in his heavy Basque accent.

"Yes! Some we made ourselves," I told him.

"You bet I'll have some," he said, pleasantly surprised.

I poured a generous amount of the wine in a tumbler before him. All eyes watched as he took a drink. He sat the glass down without saying a word. Finally, I asked, "What do you think?"

He looked at me and quietly said, "That is the worst wine I've ever tasted," which was something coming from an eighty-year-old man who drank every day since he was little. "But," he continued, "It is better than Kool-Aid!" After that day, every time Gramps came to eat (which seemed to be a little more often), he would have a glass of our first and last batch of Elderberry wine.

Years later, when Gramps was in his nineties, he was featured in *Modern Maturity* magazine, where he told his life story. When they asked Grandpa his secret to living so long, he answered, "A glass of wine with every meal."

When I read this, I chuckled and couldn't help but think that had that had been our elderberry wine he drank all those years, he never would have seen ninety.

CHAPTER 2

The Crazy Sheepherder

"Life on a ranch teaches you that truth is often stranger than fiction—and twice as memorable."

I had so many experiences working at the Paris Ranch. Of them all, the following story stands out, and I remember it as if it were yesterday.

During the winter of 1976-1977, I was nineteen. Paris' summer ranch was located seventy-five miles northwest of Ely, Nevada. The winter range where we trailed the sheep in November, which was eighty miles southwest of Ely, was one of the most desolate places on Earth. Sagebrush valleys running north and south were flanked on both sides by rough, rocky mountains dotted with juniper and pine trees.

Bert, one of the owners, and his wife Kathy spent the winter in a 1950s single-wide trailer. Behind the trailer sat a small, eight-by-sixteen-foot bunk house where groceries were stored. The small building smelled of oranges, and bunkbeds occupied one end. That was where I slept. The bunkhouse had no heat but was well insulated. Sunshine through the three large south-facing windows heated the building and usually kept it warm enough to prevent the groceries and myself from freezing at night.

A five-hundred-gallon water tank buried on the hill above gravity-fed water to the trailer. We used it sparingly since it was a long way to haul water. No matter how dirty we were, a short shower every two weeks was standard. It was a hard life. An outhouse a few yards west of camp served as our toilet. A propane stove was used for cooking meals.

Most nights, we would use two gas-powered Coleman lanterns for light, but occasionally, the diesel-powered generator was started to provide electricity. One of my least favorite jobs was hand-cranking the large metal wheel to get it started, worrying about breaking my arm if it kicked back. We had a radio but no TV, and our routine was to read for a couple of hours before bedtime.

One quiet evening, the lights of an approaching pickup shone through the window. We rarely saw vehicles during the day, let alone after dark. Two women exited the pickup. It was Tina, the wife of Thomas who was the neighboring sheep rancher, and Thomas's eighteen-year-old sister Lisa.

Their winter ranch was twenty-five miles away—our only neighbors. Cousins of Bert, the ancestors of both families, had started in the sheep business many years before. Both ranches ran around six thousand five hundred sheep at the time.

Tina and Lisa looked scared as they exited the pickup, and then Tina relayed their story.

That morning, Tina's father-in-law, Old Tom (since his son's name was Tom, this was the name he went by), and his wife Linda were on their way to town, a hundred miles away. It was winter, with a couple of inches of snow on the ground. Driving the forty miles of dirt road before finding pavement, they saw a naked man walking through the sagebrush. Not just any naked man—it was their twenty-year-old Mexican sheepherder José.

Exiting the road and driving through the sagebrush, they approached José, who continued walking and seemed oblivious to their presence. Old Tom rolled down his window and asked in Spanish, "Where are you going?"

"To the sheep," José replied.

This was another red flag as he was not only stark naked but also walking in the opposite direction of the sheep. He would have died had they not found him that morning. After he got into the pickup, Tom asked him why he wasn't dressed.

"Because your son (Thomas) told me not to wear any clothes," was his reply.

What we later discovered was that a few days prior to all of that, while taking groceries to José, Thomas told him that he should take his clothes off at night. Drying them before putting them back on the next morning would keep him warmer.

José had arrived from Mexico with a sheep-shearing crew that spring and wanted to stay and herd sheep. This was the first cold winter he had experienced. Knowing something wasn't right, Old Tom and Linda took him to his camp to get dressed and then went to the ranch to leave him there while they went to town.

José spent that day with their son Thomas, who could also see something was wrong. Accompanying him while taking provisions to one of the camps, José sat inside the pickup while Thomas delivered the groceries. The herder's horse was tied behind the camp.

When Thomas got back into the pickup, he found José agitated. José said, "Tell that guy to take the saddle off his horse." It was common practice never to leave a horse saddled when not in use.

Thomas, who spoke fluent Spanish, explained that the herder was preparing to leave. José was now livid. "If you don't tell him, I'm going to call your dad on the CB radio, and he will tell him."

Thomas then knew without a doubt that José was not all there. The sheepherder acted strange the rest of the day, but it wasn't until that night that all hell broke loose.

Everyone was in the living room after supper when José complained about his feet. Linda, who had once been a nurse, had José remove his shoes. The bottoms of his socks were caked with blood, some dried and some fresh. His feet were cut and raw from walking barefoot across the rocky ground that morning. Linda brought a pan of warm water for him to soak his feet before she cleaned them.

A couple of minutes after immersing his feet in the water, the expression on José's face changed. Suddenly, he jumped up and ran into Lisa's bedroom. Everyone looked at each other, bewildered. A minute later, José emerged from the bedroom stark naked and began chasing Tina and Lisa around the living room. Lisa ran into her bedroom with José in pursuit.

Lisa's brother Thomas was thirty at the time. He was not a big man but wiry and strong from a lifetime of work. Entering the bedroom, he grabbed José, and the fight was on. During the scuffle, José suddenly put his own index finger in his mouth and bit off the tip, fingernail and all. The scuffle moved to the floor, with Thomas sitting on José's chest, pinning his arms to the ground. "Go get Uncle Bert," Thomas told his wife and sister. "As fast as you can!"

When they arrived in a panic, Tina asked Bert's wife, Kathy, a nurse at one time herself, "Do you have anything to calm this guy down?"

"I might have some ether," Kathy replied, disappearing into the adjacent room.

Tina ran to us. "Take our pickup back to the ranch. We'll follow with Kathy in our truck."

"What the hell they need us for?" Bert asked me once she left.

"I don't know," I replied with a grin. "It might be entertaining to see a crazy man. Sure beats sitting around here reading."

It started snowing as we drove the twenty-five miles of dirt road toward the ranch. When we arrived, it was coming down hard; already three to four inches had fallen.

Tom and his family lived in an old, two-story farmhouse surrounded by a grove of cottonwoods. Exiting the pickup in the dark, I found it was dead quiet. As we walked toward the house, a scream shattered the silence. Bert and I looked at each other. I was beginning to have second thoughts about this adventure.

Linda, ashen-faced and looking much older than her fifty-five years, answered the door. "Are we ever happy to see you guys!"

Entering the house, from within, we heard another scream. We found Old Tom standing in the bedroom in shock, his gaze on Thomas who was sitting on top of the naked José as he had been for the last hour and a half. Even though the house was not warm, looking up at us, Thomas's face was covered with sweat.

As I glanced around the room, I saw the chest of drawers knocked over. Blankets were ripped off the bed, a pool of blood was smeared on the floor from Jose's bitten finger, and drops of blood were splattered on the wall where he had kicked his bloody feet. José lying there was a sight I will never forget. His thick, curly black hair seemed to stand on end, and his black eyes were as big as saucers. He looked like the devil himself.

As I walked between José and the wall, Old Tom said, "Watch him, Mike. He kicks like a mule; he's already knocked me down twice."

"What's his name?" Bert asked.

"José," Thomas replied.

Bert then asked José, *¿Cómo está?"* (How are you?). My Spanish was limited then, but I could tell by his expression and how he screamed his reply that he was not good.

"Does Kathy have anything to knock this guy out?" Old Tom muttered.

"I don't know," said Bert. "I've never seen anything like that around here."

"Maybe we could use starting fluid," I offered. We often used that to start the diesel when cold and called it ether.

"Hey, I have some of that here," Tom said as he headed out the door into the snowy night.

Soon afterward, Kathy and Tina returned, followed by Tom shaking a can of starting fluid. "What are you doing with that?" asked Kathy.

"Isn't this what you have?" questioned Tom.

"God no!" replied Kathy. "You will kill him with that!"

So much for my idea...

After we gathered in the bedroom, Kathy put a small amount of the genuine ether on a cloth. She told us it was essential to administer just a little at a time. After the fabric was removed from his nose and mouth, José's eyes became even larger, and he started screaming in Spanish. I couldn't understand much but knew what he said was not pleasant.

Bert, my boss, was Basque and fluent in that language. Throughout most of his life, they had employed Basque herders. In later years, Peruvians, Mexicans, and Chileans started taking over the herding jobs. Bert's Spanish could have been better. "What did he just say, Thomas?" asked Bert.

Thomas, very tired, turned toward us, still dripping with sweat, and replied, "He said if he gets loose, he'll kill me first and Kathy second." I secretly hoped my name was down the list far enough to get the chance to run if that should happen.

A second dose was administered, and José's ranting continued. This time, I understood since I knew all the cuss words.

"Me cago en Thomas, Me cago en Tina, Me cago en Linda."

He screamed in slang Spanish, cursing almost everyone at the ranch, declaring that he would *shit on them*. This was getting scarier by the minute. I found myself thinking how naive I had been, believing there would be any excitement, let alone fun, in seeing a crazy man. After the third dose of ether, José relaxed as the drug finally took effect.

After he went to sleep, someone brought in a large piece of canvas. We re-bandaged his finger, then carefully laid José on the material. A soft rope tied his wrists around his chest to prevent him from biting off any more fingers. From their ranch, it was one hundred miles to town, and it would be catastrophic if he should escape en route. Next, we rolled him in the canvas and secured it with four nylon straps. Kathy, who in her nursing days had seen this before, said, "I've witnessed guys like this get out of strait jackets." So we then put him in a light sleeping bag and tied it with a lariat rope.

While José slept, we went outside. The snow was still falling and, by now, ten inches deep. We shoveled out the pickup and slid a camper into the back. Coffee was poured when we returned to the warm farmhouse. Since we had no phones back then, Thomas and Tina had already taken off for town to alert the hospital.

Sitting at the table, Old Tom looked at me and asked, "How brave are you, Mike?"

I wasn't sure how to answer that question and asked, "Why?"

"Kathy and Lisa will be in the pickup, and if you ride in the back with José, you could let them know if he starts to escape."

"Why don't *you* ride in the back with José?" I countered.

"Because I have to herd his sheep in the morning," Tom told me.

"I'll ride back there with you," said Bert. At that, I reluctantly agreed.

After coffee, we picked up the sleeping José in his cloth cocoon; he awoke as we transported him to the pickup. At that point, José screamed words I wished I could, and in the same respect, glad I couldn't understand. I wondered what was going through the poor guy's mind.

After placing Jose on the camper floor, Bert, holding a flashlight, told Kathy and Lisa if José starts to get loose, he'll flash the light three times through the back window, signaling them to stop and help. We sat on benches on either side of the camper with José on the floor. It was still snowing hard as we headed for town.

The road to Ely was forty miles of dirt, then sixty miles of pavement, and Kathy was in a hurry. She hit a bump, and the unsecured camper jumped upward from the back of the pickup. Bert shined the light once into the cab. The brakes came on, hurtling us toward the front of the camper. Kathy and Lisa ran to the back, thinking José was getting loose.

Opening the door, Bert yelled, "Slow this damn thing down!" They returned to the cab without saying a word, and off we went at the same neck-breaking speed. Soon, the camper jumped into the air again. Bert's flashlight caused them to stop, and Bert hollered at them once more. Continuing, she didn't go any slower, and Bert finally gave up. Much to our relief, the camper and its contents were still in place when we reached the pavement.

We traveled in silence for the next ten miles.

José, who had been quiet, eventually said, "Untie me."

My Spanish skills were limited, but I understood this. "No!" I said.

"¿Por qué?" (Why?) he asked.

"Porque tu es un poco loco." (Because you're a little crazy.)

Bert said, "Don't tell him that; tell him he is sick or something, but don't tell him he's crazy!"

Soon, we entered the town of Ely. The street lights we passed under on the outskirts periodically illuminated the little camper. Looking down, I could see José working his fingers from the inside to pull down the material to expose his face. It was a sight unlike anything I had ever seen. Scarier than the scariest movie.

His thick black hair stood straight out from his head, the whites of his wide eyes almost glowed in the faint light, and he was staring directly at me. I raised my arm to shield his face from me and told him, "Don't look at me!" During the last mile,

I didn't glance in his direction again, terrified of what I might see.

It was late when we arrived at the hospital; a doctor, a nurse, a janitor, and Thomas and Tina were waiting for us. José was transferred to a gurney and wheeled into a room. The first thing the doctor did was prepare a syringe.

José was coherent and talked wildly in Spanish. His crazed eyes darted around the room.

The doctor gave the shot and told us a second one might be required for someone like this. A second shot did indeed need to be administered. Finally, even though he was not entirely sedated, it was enough to extract him from the homemade straight jacket. Lying on the gurney, his naked body was covered with a sheet from his chest to his ankles. Four nylon seat belts held him in place.

I was relieved our part was finished and more than ready to leave when the doctor asked if we could stay to help. Even though he was sedated, José was still awake. My assigned job was to hold down his left shoulder and head as the doctor cleaned and bandaged his finger and feet. Through the process, José screamed and ranted. I was glad not to understand most of it. I held his head in place with his greasy hair, afraid to look at him. I had the worst job of all and could smell his putrid breath as he screamed.

When the doctor finished, José finally relaxed and drifted off to sleep, exhausted. We accompanied him as he was wheeled on the gurney to his room, and what a room it was! Four walls, no window, and only a mattress on the floor. Someone asked, "Why no blanket?"

"Because he could strangle himself," was the reply.

Two sheriff deputies were assigned to the hospital for the next three days to help the doctor administer sedation. They say someone in Jose's condition has the strength of ten men. After what I witnessed, I know that to be true. Seeing his strength, I had more respect for Thomas after that day.

A week later, Bert went to town.

"Well, how's José?" I asked him when he returned.

"The outfit he came with in the spring is heading back to Mexico to recruit a shearing crew," Bert replied. "They'll take him back home."

I thought for a moment. "Without medication, what will happen if he flips out on the way there?"

Bert's response was matter-of-fact. "They'll cut his throat and leave him in a wash."

We never figured out what caused José to go insane. Perhaps the isolation, or maybe he had been fighting demons his whole life. After that experience, I hoped to never see a crazy person again. Nearly fifty years later, I still think of young José and wonder how his life turned out.

We never heard from him again.

Date Night AT THE SHEEPCAMP

CHAPTER 3

Date Night at the Sheep Camp

"Life at the sheep camp was hard, but the laughs were unforgettable—and some stories were just too wild to make up."

Louie arrived in the spring of 1977, just before the sheep were sheared. He was nineteen, my age, and accompanied by another young Guatemalan who referred to himself as Mario. The two men somehow found their way to our sheep winter range in the middle of nowhere, eighty miles from the nearest town, looking for work. They came at a good time, as two weeks later was shearing, then the fifteen-day, eighty-mile-long trail moving the sheep to the lambing range, not by trucks, but on horseback. My job involved moving camps and hauling water for the sheep on that arduous two-week journey. However, this was nothing compared to the work that needed to be done once lambing began. Two young guys willing to do this job were welcome, regardless of where they came from.

Louie was not his real name, but it was what he went by, as stated on his social security card, bought and paid for. I don't remember much about Mario, but Louie, I will never forget. He had experienced a hard life growing up in Guatemala. Short in stature, his round face showed his Indian heritage, and he was seldom without a smile.

From what I understood in my limited Spanish, getting here must have been quite a journey. The only English he knew was, "Give me one chicken, please." I'm sure as many miles as they traveled, he must have eaten a lot of chicken along the way. He was an all-right herder, not the best, but not the worst. Herding sheep took a lot of practice, and Louie might have been one of the greats had he decided to stay.

The trail and lambing (a story itself) were finished, and it was time to take the six herds of sheep to spend the summer in the high country. Once a week, I brought supplies and mail to the sheep camp above the ranch, which was Louie's. The band of sheep he tended numbered around two thousand two hundred, including the lambs. Louie lived in a tent, and I was usually the only person he saw. He had his dog and horse to keep him company.

A typical sheepherder summer camp (c. 1977)

The owner, Bert, always encouraged me to spend time with the herders, as it was a lonely life. On my visits, I tried to spend an hour or more with Louie, sometimes longer if I was moving his camp, which was done every couple of weeks to keep the sheep on fresh pasture.

One day after I delivered supplies, Louie handed me his outgoing mail. With minimal eye contact and a chuckle, he told me he needed a money order from the ranch to buy something.

"What are you ordering?" I asked.

Looking at the ground, he quietly replied, "A *muñecha*." That was a word I didn't understand, so he picked up a catalog and pointed to a picture of an inflatable doll. The magazine displayed an array of sex toys of every shape and size, and looking at the image of the doll, it seemed almost lifelike. I was speechless but smiled as he handed me the envelope. *If they are that good-looking, I might get one myself,* I thought.

The order was sent, and a couple of weeks later, Louie's package arrived. Having never seen anything like it, I couldn't wait to see the contents. With the box next to me on the seat, I drove up the rough mountain road to Louie's camp. When I handed him the package, he was embarrassed, but I encouraged him to open it while I was there, which he reluctantly did.

    When he opened the box, a face stared up at us. It was made of hard plastic; the back of the head and the body were a thin, flesh-colored plastic vinyl. The ruby red lips on the face were perfectly round, the size of a silver dollar. A plastic vinyl sac ten inches long was attached to the lips and recessed inward. Removing the doll from its box, we discovered two more plastic sacks between the doll's legs, one in the front and one in the back. She was also equipped with a hard plastic bosom. It in no way resembled the picture of that good-looking gal we saw in the catalog!

    I don't believe I ever laughed so hard in my life as we looked this thing over. Louie's sheepish grin told me he also found it amusing, but he never said a word. I unloaded the groceries and hurriedly left to give Louie and his new girlfriend some alone time. I laughed all the way back to the ranch.

    After that day, during my weekly visits, the doll was never mentioned again. At the end of the summer, I prepared to move Louie's camp to the ranch, where the lambs would be shipped to market and the ewes worked to start preparing them for their long journey to the winter range. Louie was bringing the sheep off the mountain and wasn't there when I packed his belongings that afternoon. On the floor of the tent, there was the box.

    I knew I shouldn't do it, but I couldn't help myself. Curious about the fate of the doll, I opened the top and peered inside. Without touching it, I could clearly see it had been well used. The plastic that was once flesh-colored and shiny was now scuffed and dirty. It had been a while since Louie had given her a good bath; that was all I needed to see and quickly closed the box.

    Then, I noticed a couple of dirty magazines. Being nineteen years old, it was natural to thumb through the pages. What I saw next shocked me. Louie had written people's names on every naked person's body in the photos of a nudist camp magazine. Names of people from the ranch and even a couple of the other herders were identified in the photographs. My eyes widened, and my mouth fell open when I saw a photo of two guys lathering each other up in the shower with the names "Mike" and "Louie" written beneath them. I couldn't burn the magazines in the fire pit fast enough.

I then loaded the camp and moved everything to the ranch, thankful the summer was over and my weekly camp-tending days for Louie were finished. I would still have to occasionally tend his camp, but from then on, my visits were short and sweet.

Later that fall, Louie and Mario headed out for parts unknown, hopefully, to find some real women! Leaving me with an unforgettable memory of the shower pictures at the nudist camp. It was embarrassing back then, and I saw no humor in it. However, looking back now, I can't help but smile.

Ten years later, I was a government trapper, hunting/trapping coyotes south of Wendover, Nevada. Thirty-four thousand sheep from Utah wintered there. At the time, I was living in a camp wagon close to a remote highway maintenance station. One day, I walked into the garage and heard laughter. Four workers were looking at an inflatable doll they had found along the highway and had just finished blowing it up with an air compressor. Talk about a blast from the past! It was a twin to Louie's doll, and what memories it rekindled. I joined in the laughter and told them the story from years before.

Twenty miles to the south was a flock of three thousand ewes that belonged to two brothers. When water needed to be hauled to the sheep, they both stayed in the small sheepwagon. When snow was on the ground, providing moisture for the sheep, the brothers could take weekly turns going to Utah to spend time with their families.

Lee, one of the brothers, was a big, good-natured man and a special friend. Some of the best lamb I ever ate cooked on a sheepwagon stove was at his camp.

One night, I came up with an idea. Early the next morning, I went into the shop, re-inflated the doll with the compressor, and placed it in the passenger seat of my pickup. It was only a mile of highway to the turnoff that took me the twenty-five miles of rough dirt road to Lee's camp. There wasn't much traffic, especially at that time of day, but I was ready to hide the doll if I saw another vehicle. What an embarrassment that would have been if I had gone around a corner and seen someone I knew who wanted to visit. Fortunately, I made it to Lee's camp unseen.

I knew he'd be with the sheep that time of day, so I went into the sheepwagon and placed the doll in his bed. I covered her bottom half, and what a sight that was. The hard plastic face, bosom, and vinyl arms pointed toward the ceiling, looking like the doll was lying in bed waiting for Lee's return. I was laughing so hard when I left that I almost fell out of the sheepwagon door.

The next day, when I visited Lee's camp, he was waiting. He knew who was responsible and did not find it nearly as funny as I did. "Where's the doll?" I asked.

"In the bottom of a mine shaft," was his reply. Then he continued (and I *think* he was joking), "If my wife would have made a surprise visit and found that thing in my bed, you might have found yourself down there with it."

CHAPTER 4

A Brand-New Life

*"Every journey has a turning point;
mine came through hard work, heartbreak, and finally
landing the job I had dreamed of."*

For nearly two years, I worked at the Paris Ranch. It was an enormous operation in rural Eastern Nevada that ran over six thousand sheep and eight hundred mother cows north and south of Ely. Every day, we worked hard from daylight until dark; luckily, life slowed down when the sheep were in the winter range. It was at that time that I practiced becoming a trapper.

Over those two winters, I caught numerous bobcats, gray foxes, and coyotes and even captured my fingers a few times. Oh, how I loved to trap; whether I trapped anything or not didn't matter. Simply being outdoors and learning from experience was reward enough.

I had previously submitted my application to the State of Nevada. During those years, in Nevada, all trappers were employed by the state, and most of the supervisors were federal. Not a day went by that I didn't dream of getting that job. I received several letters from the department notifying me they had filled a position, saying I wasn't successful due to my lack of experience. However, I continued to gain that experience daily and never gave up hope.

In the spring of 1978, after we sheared the sheep, one of my closest friends on the ranch was unloading a bulldozer and was tragically killed at the young age of twenty-three. Even though it's been almost fifty years, the memory stays fresh. The feelings of loss and sadness I felt are difficult to put into words.

After the funeral, we began the long journey trailing the sheep north to the lambing range eighty miles away. The herders followed the large flocks on horseback while I stayed busy hauling water for the sheep and moving their camps. The hard work helped distract my mind, but it was a sad time for us all. I was twenty years old.

When we arrived at the lambing range two weeks later, the state trapper assigned to help us with coyotes drove to my camp to tell me that Mike Laughlin, the supervisor for Animal Damage Control (later known as USDA Wildlife Services), had granted me an interview. Hearing the news was just what I needed to lift my spirits. I might not get the position, but now I finally had a chance. The grueling job of lambing wouldn't begin for a couple of days; it was the end of April, a perfect time to meet with him before the real work began.

I left early and headed for my hometown of McGill, just north of Ely. My interview with Mike was scheduled for 1 p.m. What a hectic and eventful day that was. At my folks' place, washing off a month's worth of filth, I took a much-needed shower that lasted an hour.

I had met Mike Laughlin before. He was a straightforward person whom employees revered or feared, depending on how you did your job. He kept things in order and ran a tight ship. I remember very little of the interview that day. I was nervous, but I must have said the right things because, in the end, I was offered the job I had so long wished for.

It was one of the happiest moments of my life. The job was not full-time but a six-month appointment. In those days, the government gave each western state funding to hire two part-time employees for the busy spring and summer months. They allocated that money for several years after banning toxicants in 1972, previously used to kill coyotes.

If I proved myself, it could become a full-time job.

But there was a problem.

I had to start work the following week.

Upon hearing the news, a sick feeling crept into my stomach. "Lambing begins in a couple of days," I carefully said.

"I can't abandon the ranch right now, especially after they just lost a member of the family."

Mike remained silent, his gaze on me.

"Could I start in three weeks? When lambing has slowed?"

He looked at me in silence. The man's steely gaze was unwavering. I felt that I had just lost my chance. Finally, he said, "How does June 5 sound?"

I was stunned.

The decision surprised me as not only were we starting to lamb, but so were many others. Given the season, I knew he needed me now.

Years later, I asked Mike why he hired me that day. He said, "I figured anyone that would work like you did and show that much dedication at the end would be a good employee."

After returning to the ranch, I told Bert about the interview. Though I knew he wasn't thrilled to see me go, I could tell he was relieved that I would stay to help through the worst of lambing. There were no congratulations or smiles. That's just the way he was.

As we both got up to leave, Bert paused and asked, "You'll need a horse for your new job, won't you?" I nodded. "Go pick out whichever horse you want and use it as long as you need it." He then turned and walked away.

Lambing started and kept me occupied with unrelenting work. It was the old way, horseback, lambing over six thousand sheep in the open. Perhaps twenty people worked there at lambing time, sleeping in simple conditions, sheepwagons, and in an old bus with bunk beds on one end. The sagebrush was our bathroom. Our days started before dawn and ended after dark, except for the night herders who worked from dusk 'til dawn. There was no going to town, no baths, just focusing on getting through each day to help every lamb survive.

Lambing time is a story in itself, and the days passed one by one. Then, on June 3, it came time for me to leave. Everyone was busy, and the goodbyes would come later. I slowly drove away that day, knowing this was the beginning of my brand-new life.

On June 5, 1978, I loaded my horse in the back of the pickup. A narrow horse rack made of pipe was bolted to the center of the bed. In front of the rack, a half-circle windbreak shielded the horse from the wind and bugs during travel. Mel Anderson, the supervisor from Ely, had set up a sheepwagon for me to live in on Spruce Mountain, seventy-five miles north of McGill, and was waiting there for me when I arrived.

Until I started work that day, he had been covering for me. Mel spent the next few days showing me the expansive lambing range and introducing the sheepherders on the Sorenson Ranch. There they lambed out around five thousand sheep from the first of May until later in June. I would work ten days on and four days off, protecting the young lambs from coyotes and assisting the federal lion hunter Dick Hall when mountain lions attacked.

The job was what I'd always dreamed of. Very few twenty-year-olds today would be happy living under such conditions, but I was not bothered. I was used to solitude; the loneliness didn't affect me. On my four days off, I'd go to McGill to see my family, take a much-needed shower, and enjoy some home-cooked meals or visit my second family at the Paris Ranch. During work days, the Peruvian herders on Spruce Mountain kept me company, and my Spanish improved.

I had been working for two weeks but still had not met my supervisor from Elko until the evening the helicopter landed at my camp. We were going to hunt coyotes early the following morning, so Mitch, the supervisor, and Ted, the pilot, were there to spend the night at my camp.

Mike with Peruvian herders

The first person I saw exit the helicopter was a young man in his twenties. From what I could see, he didn't look old enough to be a pilot. The second one was a grizzled old trapper type. I certainly hoped the young guy was a good pilot, but as it turned out, I had their roles reversed.

Mitch, my supervisor, was in his twenties and, like myself, had started young. He had been a trapper for five years and, during that time, had accumulated countless hours gunning coyotes from a Super Cub airplane and helicopters before his promotion to supervisor. Little did I know then that I had met a lifelong friend. Ted has since passed, but forty-seven years later, Mitch and his wife Clayre remain good friends.

Flying in the helicopter hunting coyotes was what I had long dreamed of. At daylight the next morning, as the helicopter rose above the treetops, I could see everything and was sure the coyotes didn't stand a chance. However, fifteen minutes later, flying over the band of sheep that the coyotes had been killing, I discovered the process wasn't nearly as simple as I had imagined.

As the helicopter made a sudden left turn, the pilot called out, "One, two, three, four coyotes!"

Where? I thought, looking below, seeing nothing but sagebrush and juniper trees. Then, four small brown dots appeared, running away from the ewes and little lambs, much smaller than I had anticipated. Ted skillfully maneuvered the helicopter from one coyote to the other at telephone pole height, and in a matter of minutes, it was over. Mitch's shooting was one of the most impressive shows I'd ever seen. Countless lambs were saved by removing those four coyotes. That morning's flight reinforced my thoughts about what a great job I had.

My school was just beginning, and there was much more to learn. From the lambing range, I was sent to work on the Idaho border near Jarbidge, Nevada, at the end of June. There, many bands of sheep grazed the lush mountainsides during the summer months.

My constant companions in that remote camp were my horse and dog. My work schedule consisted of hunting and trapping coyotes five days a week on horseback. Being alone in the mountains, one hundred miles from town, I needed to be careful. It was there I began the second semester of my formal education.

How else was I supposed to learn such things? There were no schools that taught the trade. I compared my job to the Army. They told me when I started, "We will teach you," and they did!

Buzz in the Sudzz

CHAPTER 5

Buzz in the Sudzz

"Some lessons you learn in the air, others on the ground—but with Buzz, you got both."

In early October 1978, five months after starting my career with Wildlife Services, I was stationed in Battle Mountain, Nevada, to live in a camp trailer in the middle of nowhere. The area was a vast winter range that, in those years, was home to many bands of sheep from October through April. I mainly ran traps but also shot coyotes threatening the sheep.

One Monday morning, I was called to the office in Elko, seventy miles away. The assistant state supervisor, Mike Laughlin, surprised me with a big question.

"How would you like to hunt coyotes from the airplane?"

I had just turned twenty-one, was single, and looking for adventure, so I quickly said yes. He told me to meet Buzz, the airplane pilot, at the Battle Mountain Airport the following day and try it. I was excited and nervous at the same time. I had watched them hunt from the plane before, but I had never thought I would have the chance to do it myself. Until then, the only flight I had ever made was a round trip from Ely to Reno on United.

It was a small airport, and I anxiously awaited Buzz's arrival early the next afternoon. Soon, a small yellow airplane appeared from the north: a Super Cub. After landing, it taxied to the gas pump, and the door opened. An older man, of about seventy, exited the plane. His face reminded me of Droopy, the cartoon character with long, sagging cheeks; he introduced himself as Buzz.

He gave me a tour of the small plane. The cockpit was tight and narrow, with two seats: one in front where the pilot sat and one directly behind for the gunner. I could see that I wouldn't have to extend my elbows very far to touch each side of the cabin when seated. Buzz pointed to the shooting window on the left and showed me how it functioned. He next showed me the strut attaching the wing to the bottom of the plane and the tire located beneath the window.

Super Cub

"I won't be happy if you shoot either of those while chasin' coyotes," he said.

I needed to be aware of two other hazards: the fuel tank on the wing's leading edge above the window and the propeller in front, which was invisible when turning and could be shot if I wasn't careful.

While he refueled the plane, Buzz had me practice getting in and out of the back seat, which was simpler said than done. Next, I rehearsed putting the shotgun in and out of the left shooting window and paid close attention to the obstacles previously mentioned. That was part one of my aerial gunning training. Then, it was time to hunt coyotes.

After we took off and I was settled into the back seat of the small plane, Buzz lit a cigarette, filling the small cab with smoke. (This was before smoking was banned in airplanes and helmets and proper training weren't required.) He informed me that we would go south of the airport a few miles for some practice shots. It was a dry fall, and he thought I could shoot at rocks and use the dust to see where I hit.

After flying the short distance, I spotted a coyote running through the sagebrush. "There's a coyote," I hollered at Buzz. Back then, there were no helmets or intercom systems like today, only ball caps. Tapping his shoulder, I pointed, showing him the coyote.

"What do you want to do?" he yelled.

"We can practice on this one," I shouted back.

The plane circled around and leveled, heading toward the running coyote. I double-checked the location of the tire, strut, gas tank, and invisible propeller. At the height of a telephone pole, we flew over the coyote faster than it could run. With the semi-automatic shotgun, I fired two shots in rapid succession. The coyote kept running, but I could see by the dust from my shots that I had hit close. This was the most exciting thing I had ever done.

The plane banked, making a turn so sharp I could watch the coyote through the plexiglass skylight on the aircraft's roof. Leveling off, on the next pass, I got him. I had always heard how difficult shooting from the plane was and remarked to Buzz, "That wasn't bad!" The following two coyotes went like the first, and I shouted, "This isn't near as tough as they say."

Buzz told me, "Be careful. It's not as easy as you think."

On the fifth coyote, I began missing.

I missed the first pass, the second, and then the third. The harder I tried, the worse I shot. Pass after pass, the coyote kept running. Two boxes of shells later, the coyote finally fell over, and I don't think it was because of what I was attempting to do but instead caused by pure exhaustion. Buzz didn't say a word but turned and looked at me sideways with a slight grin, as if to say, "I told you so."

Buzz had flown for many years. I didn't know much about his past except he had been a mustanger. With the plane, he'd herd wild horses toward riders hidden in trees. The horsemen would then push them into wings constructed of tree limbs that narrowed into a corral. He told me he would sometimes have a bottle hidden, land, and have a shot—"Those were the good ol' days." He had only flown a short time for us and was a contract pilot, charging so much an hour for his services. The government also helped reimburse his meals and board.

Buzz, however, had two problems.

He couldn't see well and liked to drink.

I flew a couple more times with Buzz, and it became easier with practice. One morning at the Elko office, Mike Laughlin asked, "Well, how do you like flying?"

"Great!" I replied enthusiastically. It was the truth.

"Good, so how would you like to become a full-time gunner for the rest of winter?"

In the airplane, we'd respond to sheep depredations all over the northwestern corner of Nevada. Young, single, and fearless at the time (fearless and stupid can sometimes be synonymous when you're that age), I jumped at the chance. Buzz would fly the plane to whatever town we would work out of next. I would bring my pickup with our luggage and whatever items were needed for the plane. After three or four days, it was on to the next location.

The winter of 1978-79 was frigid. There were no hangers, so we tied up outside. Many mornings, we had to brush heavy frost from the wings with a push broom. We had wedged a hundred-watt lightbulb next to the engine the night before for heat and plugged the holes in the cowling with loose insulation. A piece of cardboard was placed over the windshield and skylight to keep frost from forming. This experience made me greatly appreciate the hangers we had available in later years.

The starter on the old canary yellow Super Cub didn't work well in the cold. At times, Buzz would have to hand-crank the propeller while I held the brakes from the back seat. Scared to death, I secretly worried the plane would take off once it started and cut Buzz to shreds like something out of an Indiana Jones movie.

Buzz knew the country well. He would coordinate our flight plans with the bosses regarding where and when we were needed next. That winter, I saw a lot of country and stayed in almost every town in northwest Nevada. Buzz especially loved flying out of a small place north of Winnemucca. There, he owned a single-wide trailer where he would spend part of his summers. When we stayed there, he would get per diem (meal rate) and could make a little extra money with home-cooked meals.

Every evening at the motel, Buzz pulled a half-gallon bottle of Vodka from his suitcase and had a few drinks. Vodka mixed with water was his drink of choice. When we went out to eat, he would have a couple more. I knew he drank a lot, but he seemed to be able to handle it. He told me once that in his horse-wrangling days, he could fly better after a drink or two than most could sober. Other than not seeing well, he was an excellent pilot and still flying at seventy, so I had no reason to doubt him.

While flying out of Winnemucca one day, Buzz received a call from a sheepman to the north asking if he could search for lost sheep. We started flying at daylight most mornings, so were done by early afternoon. After we finished hunting the following day, Buzz refueled the plane, and we hunted north. We would meet the sheepman in the same small town where Buzz kept his trailer. It had been quite some time since we had flown out of there, as the bosses told Buzz that no problems had occurred.

Landing at the small airport that afternoon, we noticed a helicopter parked on the side of the runway with a pickup alongside it. Our contract helicopter was there with one of the bosses and another employee offloading coyotes into the pickup. In those years, coyotes were worth a lot of money, so we salvaged many of them to help pay for the flying.

When Buzz saw this, he was infuriated. Here was the boss, and all this time, he had told Buzz there was no flying to be done in the area.

They looked sheepish as we walked up to them. I could cut the tension with a knife. They knew they had been caught and that Buzz was pissed. Very few words were spoken and it was an awkward situation. Thankfully, the rancher arrived about that time. Buzz returned to the plane and I stayed behind to help skin coyotes.

A couple of hours later, I jumped into the back seat of the plane, and we headed for Winnemucca. That night, Buzz drank more than usual. He informed me the plane needed a one-hundred-hour service and that we could not fly for a day or two. I thought it strange that he hadn't mentioned this before.

I called my supervisor (not the same one from the helicopter episode) that evening to inform him about the one-hundred-hour service. He said our other helicopter would fly out of a small-town east of us, and he wanted me to accompany them the next morning as a spotter. That sounded better than sitting in a motel room, so I relayed the plan to Buzz. He'd had a few drinks by then and was madder than I had ever seen him.

"Go ahead. I will see you when you get back," he said. He hated helicopters to begin with and now hated them even more.

Early the following day, I met the helicopter, and after flying, I stayed the night. We flew again the next morning, and afterward, I headed to Winnemucca, hoping the scheduled service had been completed. It was 1 p.m. when I arrived at the motel. Knocking on Buzz's door, I got no answer; I knocked louder.

Finally, Buzz opened the door, dressed only in shorts and looking terrible. Upon entering his dark room, I realized it had not been cleaned since I left. I spotted two empty vodka bottles. Buzz lay down on the bed and said, "Mike, I need help."

"What can I do?" I asked.

Buzz responded, "I need to dry out; take me to the hospital." I grabbed his suitcase and loaded it along with Buzz into my pickup.

We soon arrived at the hospital on the south side of town. After admitting Buzz, I drove back to the motel, not knowing what to do next or how long my pilot might be in detox. After an hour, I headed back to the hospital to see how he was doing. Halfway there, I found Buzz on the street, walking away from the hospital.

I stopped and asked, "What are you doing?"

As he clambered into the pickup, he told me, "You ring for a nurse, you ring for a nurse, and they don't come, so I left."

Once at the motel, I walked Buzz to his room.

"Come in and have a drink," he said.

"Oh, maybe later."

My pilot was drunk, and the scheduled service had yet to be started. Wondering what to do next, I walked to my room and made perhaps the toughest call of my young life. I told my boss what was happening. I knew this would end Buzz's flying career with us, but I had no choice. My supervisor, Mike, instructed me to leave in the morning. It was time to go back to trapping.

I decided to wait until the next day to relay the information to Buzz. He looked worse than the night before. I told him my plans.

"What do I do now?" he asked glumly.

I didn't know what to say and finally told him, "I think that's a question only you can answer."

After that day, I never saw Buzz again or ever heard of what happened to him. A year later, I transferred to Wyoming and then to Montana. I know he never flew for the program again.

Years later, I searched for Buzz on the computer, both in the town where he lived and where his trailer was located. I found no obituary or any information to show the man had ever existed. None of my co-workers, not even the bosses I talked to afterward, knew anything about Buzz or what had happened to him. It was like he'd disappeared without a trace, leaving me with a feeling like I had been flying with a ghost.

CHAPTER 6

David the Wilderness Chef

"Out here, every mistake is a lesson, and every meal earned is a feast worth remembering."

I learned to be a prepper early in life; I had to. Of course, this didn't happen overnight. It required many tough lessons while working at the remote Paris Ranch, and later trapping in rural Nevada, Wyoming, and Montana. I was often alone in the middle of nowhere and always planned for worst-case scenarios.

Pickups were unreliable in those days, and there were no cell phones. I worked ten days on and four off during my first summer with WS (Wildlife Services) in 1978. Part of that job was running horseback traplines for coyotes in the remote mountains near Jarbidge, Nevada. My only human contact was an occasional sheepherder. Other than that, I was by myself and often wondered what would happen if I had a horse accident and broke my leg on the first day. On day eleven, someone might think, "Where's Mike?" and then have no idea where to even begin searching.

After surviving that first summer in Jarbidge, I spent the following summer in the Ruby Mountains south of Elko, Nevada, living in a camp trailer on a remote ranch. I rode horseback four days a week, and the longest trapline, Boulder Creek, took ten hours to complete. It wasn't only coyotes that bothered the sheep; mountain lions were also a problem.

Chef David near his sheepwagon

In late June, I rode into Boulder Creek with Dick, the federal lion hunter, to meet with a sheepherder. The camptender informed us that the sheepherder had claimed he saw a lion near the sheep two days earlier.

After we rode through the creek crossing on Second Boulder, Dick pointed to a canvas bag wrapped in heavy plastic hanging from a tree. He told me it was a survival kit that included a frying pan, cooking oil, a fishing line, and fish hooks. The Boulder Creeks were full of brook trout and, due to their remote location, were seldom fished. I made note of the information, in case I got stranded.

In September, sagehen—also known as sage-grouse—season opened, and during that time of my life, one of my greatest enjoyments was hunting birds.

One evening, I drove to a meadow a couple of miles east of my camp that held many sagehens. Not long after leaving my pickup on that beautiful fall afternoon and walking a short distance, ten birds rose before me. I shot, and one fell into the tall grass. Running ahead to collect my prize, I was surprised to find the biggest sagehen I'd ever seen. It was huge! The smaller ones were the best to eat, but that didn't matter. I was happy to be twenty-one, have the best job ever, and be out hunting on an incredible fall evening.

Finding no other birds, I headed for the pickup. Nearby was a sheep camp that belonged to David. He was the only Basque sheepherder left on the large ranch. All the other herders were Peruvians. David, a big man in his early sixties, was known far and wide for his cooking skills. I was lucky enough to share some incredible meals with this man. His salted cod fish was to die for. Thinking he was probably tired of constantly eating mutton, I thought I'd surprise him with the sagehen I just shot.

It was late when I pulled up to the camp, and David stood at the doorway in a T-shirt with his curly gray hair standing out above his tanned face. "I've got something for you," I told him, proudly reaching into the pickup and lifting the large sagehen (which looked more like a turkey) from the back.

David asked, "What are you going to do with that?"

"I thought you might want it," was my reply.

"You can't eat that," he said with a Basque accent. I stopped, not knowing what to do next. David then said without enthusiasm, "If you clean it, I'll do something." I hurriedly ran to the creek in the fading light to clean my bird.

Summer was gone, and my time at the ranch was ending. In a short time, the sheep would leave for the winter range. I saddled my horse two days after visiting David's camp and headed to Boulder Creek for one final trip. That morning, I thought it would be fun to stop at Second Boulder, retrieve the survival sack, and catch some fish to eat, rather than pack a lunch as I usually did.

It was early afternoon, and I was starving when I arrived at the crossing. I unsaddled my horse and grabbed the survival sack. The first thing was to start a fire and get coals to cook over. The sack's contents revealed a frying pan, spatula, fork, jar of oil, salt and pepper, a spool of fishing line, and fishhooks. There were plenty of grasshoppers to serve as bait. I was shocked to discover this survival kit in the middle of nowhere contained no matches. I'm sure they figured anyone this far from civilization would be smart enough to have their own matches.

Mike with brook trout from Boulder Creek on one of his better days

Being lean and weighing only a hundred and fifty pounds, getting hungry didn't take much. Desperate for something to eat, I gathered dry grass and twigs. Using my eyeglasses, I tried the magnifying glass trick of condensing sunlight, making it hot enough to start a fire, but that failed. Next was the Boy Scout method of rubbing two sticks together, with the same disappointing results. Finally admitting defeat, I packed everything into the sack and hung it on the tree. Mounting my horse, I wished I had brought something to eat.

Late that afternoon, I rode off the mountain. My camp was still a couple of miles away. I spotted David's sheepwagon across the meadow. I was starving and knew I'd find a piece of bread to tie me over there. David was tending the sheep, but he wouldn't mind if I helped myself to something to eat, especially under the circumstances. I dismounted my horse and spotted the black cast-iron Dutch oven under the camp. Herders frequently put these in the shade to store their meals. Opening the lid, I wasn't disappointed. There I found the big bomber (what they used to call an old rooster sagehen). David had cooked it along with potatoes, onion, and garlic. My mouth watered as I brought the Dutch oven inside the camp and eagerly grabbed a plate and fork. Not bothering to heat it up, I filled my plate. My meal was completed with bread, cheese, and a tin cup of red wine.

Frying potatoes, Ruby Mountains, Nevada

I learned a valuable lesson that day. From then on, I always carried matches, and taking lunch became standard. Who said those old birds weren't fit to eat? That was one of the best meals I ever had in my life.

CHAPTER 7

The Hutterites

"The coyotes were just the beginning—what I discovered at the colony was so much more than I ever expected."

The Hutterite Colony in Western Montana

I almost didn't include this chapter because it differs slightly from the others. However, it explains the importance of the program and the purpose of my chosen profession. It depicts ranchers' frustration dealing with predators and, in this case, reveals how people with limited means protect themselves. Thanks to our agency's assistance in removing problem predators, promoting non-lethal methods, and the colony's support, we were able to find a solution.

Hutterite: only a handful of people know that word. The first time I heard about them was in 1982. I was a government trapper in eastern Montana. One day, a friend there told me he was going to a Hutterite colony in the western part of the state to purchase pigs. I was intrigued. "What do you mean by colony? Is this some sort of cult?" I asked.

He assured me it was not and then explained that they were a religious group that spoke German among themselves and lived on communal farms, similar to the Amish. He said they were good, hardworking people. Little did I know then what a big part of my life they would later become.

Ten years later, in April 1992, I transferred to western Montana, north of Great Falls. The area was home to several colonies, and west of where I lived was one with a large sheep operation. A coworker told me they had recently been involved in a court battle. Apparently, on colony property, someone had picked up a dead coyote and an eagle they thought were poisoned and turned them in. The authorities, who believed the Hutterites had laced sheep carcasses with poison, then removed several dead sheep from their pasture and tested them for toxins; none were found. Eventually, the court case was settled.

Since they could not prove the colony was responsible (and there was no evidence that they were), the issue was resolved with a fine and a plea of no contest. The Hutterites' lawyer advised them it would cost more to fight in court than to pay the fine.

Several days after settling into my new home, a colony member telephoned and, in a German accent, explained that coyotes had killed a sheep. Hearing the news, I became excited yet nervous. Now, I would see firsthand what these colonies were about.

Driving west that morning, I approached the top of a hill that overlooked a green basin. The colony buildings were surrounded by a treeless prairie that extended to the impressive snow-capped Rockies towering five miles to the west. (Little did I know then the future adventures I would experience in the country before me—not only with coyotes but also with wolves and grizzlies.) It was a magnificent sight to behold!

Slowly entering the colony, I observed large barns that housed dairy cows, pigs, sheep, chickens, and machine and carpenter shops. Three identical rows of houses stood in dormitory fashion. In front of each was an outhouse, but they weren't ordinary outhouses; these were heated and had lights. It would be several years before the colony built new homes and upgraded to indoor plumbing.

Inside the house was a small kitchen with a long table. In the corner was an ice box that required a block of ice from the big kitchen. A large room with numerous beds along the wall was attached.

I later learned the Hutterites ate together in one spacious dining room, so little was required in their living quarters. Church was held every day of the week. Radio and TV were not allowed, and taking pictures was frowned upon. They lived a simple, hardworking life and had everything they required.

When I pulled in, I saw ten men standing around the various buildings, all staring at me. Given everything they had recently been through, my arrival in a government pickup made them suspicious. Finally, a kindly-looking gentleman with a short gray beard but no mustache walked toward my pickup. He appeared to be in his fifties, dressed in black with a straw hat like the other men. He was physically fit with broad, prominent shoulders. In a soft voice, he introduced himself as Jake, the second preacher.

Every colony had a male secretary who oversaw the finances and helped guide the daily operations; he was often called the boss. The two preachers conducted the evening church services and the extended Sunday church while also playing a significant role in running the colony. Jake, the younger of the two, was the one who had called me.

Jake's son, Ben, was the sheepman overseeing the colony's thousand-plus ewes. Ben was in town that day, so Jake jumped into my pickup to guide me to the latest kill. On our way, he explained that the coyotes were so bad they were considering selling the sheep.

"We used to turn out the ewes with the lambs in the spring," he said. "A few coyote kills were expected." He sighed. "But with each passing year, there are more and more coyotes. We've even been bedding the sheep down close to the colony, but the coyotes are making it difficult to stay in business."

Colony members were prohibited to own or use firearms, so they had no way to defend themselves against the predators.

Mike, Ben, and Tim (2011)

Their solution to the problem was to lamb in January. They weaned the lambs at a young age, feeding them to a certain weight and never allowing them to leave the barns or corrals. Then, only the ewes were turned out to pasture the first part of May. Coyotes seldom killed ewes when lambs were present; but now they were, which is what Jake was about to show me.

We drove a mile west of the colony to the location of a sheep skeleton with tufts of white wool scattered around it. Part of my new job was grizzly bear work, and seeing how this two-hundred-pound ewe was wholly consumed, I first thought a bear might be the culprit. "When was this killed?" I asked Jake.

"Last night," he told me.

"Do you think coyotes could eat this much in one night?" I asked.

"Yes," replied Jake. "You can't believe how many coyotes are around here."

Examining the evidence, I determined that he was right. He then told me coyotes had killed forty ewes the previous year.

I had access to a Super Cub airplane and a helicopter to hunt coyotes. Looking around at the rolling grasslands, I could see that this place would be much easier to hunt in than the sagebrush-covered ground in Nevada or the badland breaks of Eastern Montana and Wyoming. I couldn't wait to get started.

I drove to the sheep barn early the following day and was greeted by Ben. I don't remember anyone happier to see me than Ben was. Like his father, Ben was in great physical shape. His beard was the same, but instead of gray, it was brown. He had some of the kindest yet most intelligent eyes I had ever seen. I later discovered he was married, as single, unbaptized men in the colony remained beardless. He was in his twenties and had recently taken over as sheep boss. His uncle previously held that job but had passed away a few months before at a young age, and Ben was chosen to replace him. Throughout his life, and in the short time he had been in charge, he had witnessed the damage coyotes could cause. Any type of help was more than welcome.

We drove west toward the kill site where Ben showed me the three large sheep pastures, explaining more about their operation. Although Hutterites first arrived in the United States in 1874, this colony had been built in 1948, as an expansion from another colony in Canada. In Ben's younger years, when not in school, he had taken turns (along with the other young boys) helping in all aspects of the colony. He spent a year or so helping with the sheep and possibly the same amount of time with the dairy, beef, hogs, or some other branch.

Every summer, farming had to be done. All the while, he went wherever help was needed. In time, each of the boys knew every part of the diverse operations of this large farm. The girls, clothed in long dresses and shawls, were taught the essential skills of sewing, cooking, and cleaning at a young age and were always ready to assist in any way needed. It's unfortunate that young people, on the outside, don't have this opportunity to learn these skills and develop such a strong work ethic. Even though formal schooling only went to eighth grade, the Hutterites were some of the most intelligent, hardworking people I knew. More impressive was the fact of how happy and close-knit the families were. They had problems like anyone, but a more joyful, better group of people would be hard to find.

That first day, I set foot-hold traps on the outside corners of the sheep pasture. The following day, I called in and shot a coyote near where the ewe had been killed. Later that morning, Ben accompanied me to check the trapline; overnight, we had captured four coyotes.

Aerial hunting over the next couple weeks, I flew first with the airplane and then with the helicopter. I thinned the coyotes out and knew I was making headway; we noticed now when they killed, it took longer to consume the carcass. Never in my career had I seen a place with so many coyotes.

Finally, flying around the sheep with the airplane one morning, I shot eight coyotes. I'm unsure which coyote or coyotes were responsible, but whatever I did that day stopped the killing.

After that morning, coyotes would still kill an occasional ewe, so I maintained a short trapline around the sheep pasture. When checking traps, Ben accompanied me as his schedule permitted. During those visits, I gained a deeper understanding of colony life. Afterward, I would often have lunch with him and the rest of the colony in the large dining hall. Ben, his wife Mary, their three young children, and many other colony members became like family.

The trapline was utilized for many years, capturing coyotes and saving countless sheep. Then, over time, the grizzly bear population exploded, and wolves appeared. The colony was forced to build electric fence bedgrounds to remain in the sheep business. It was a great tool, but much time and expense were involved to corral the sheep every evening and let them out each morning. With Wildlife Services' help, the colony added Turkish Kangel guard dogs. The killing slowed.

Afterward, we occasionally flew for coyotes when they caused problems. The colony contributed funds for flying on top of the fifty cents per head they paid yearly for predator control on each sheep. This was genuinely a cooperative effort.

Over the years, I watched Ben's family grow to eight children. My wife, Maureen, and I were fortunate to experience many events that an outsider would never see.

Ben's parents, siblings, and family still gather whenever we visit. We've had many get-togethers in their home—special times, without the distractions of TV or other technology. They all adore Maureen. One of the first times she went there, she helped the colony women process one thousand two hundred chickens. She was the first outsider ever to do so. Since then, I believe they prefer her company more than mine.

Our friend Ben has a wealth of knowledge and is always there with advice no matter what project or problem. He eventually went from sheep boss to secretary of the colony.

There are many ways to get an education, eighth grade or not; Ben's intelligence surpasses anyone I know.

The first day I met Ben, I came home and told my wife, "I met a friend today." No truer words have ever been spoken. Our families have been through so much together and remain the best of friends.

When we visit the colony, we frequently spend time at the sheep barn. When Ben left, his nephew took over as sheep boss. Mike and his helpers do a great job. While watching the lambs run and play, I can't help but be happy knowing that thirty years later, I was a small part of this.

Wolf predation, moved to one location, seventeen sheep in one night (2001)

CHAPTER 8

The Visiting Eye Doctor

"No training manual prepares you for the moments when a bear encounter turns into a headline-worthy adventure you'll never forget."

During the summer of 1994, I started calling myself a bear trapper (kind of, sort of). There were no bear-trapping schools. You learned from others, the bears, and your own mistakes. Sometimes, there's a fine line between a mistake and a fatal mistake.

A good friend of mine, Wayvan, owned a beautiful ranch at the base of the Rocky Mountains. The land was creek-bottom, surrounded by grass-covered coulees and scattered groves of willows. Wayvan was Cree Indian, a few years older than myself, and in his late thirties. He was a large man—approximately three hundred pounds—with a sense of humor as big as he was. Always fun to be around, our friendship was one that lasted for many years.

Sheep had been a part of that place for a long time. Wayvan's dad had worked for the previous owner, Ross, who was mauled by a grizzly. The bear attack didn't happen at the ranch which, for many years, had no bears except in the mountainous summer range miles away.

While checking the sheep, Ross stumbled upon a massive grizzly feeding on a ewe it had recently killed. He shot the bear and it immediately went down. As he approached, the supposedly dead bear jumped up and attacked. No other shells remained in the gun. Ross, defenseless against the attack, was severely injured. During the mauling, part of his scalp was torn off, and the bear bit him on the face. He survived but was permanently disfigured for the remainder of his life. Wayvan's dad eventually ended up with the place. Wayvan told me he had never thought of bears being around the ranch while growing up. However, they were there now.

Early one morning, Wayvan called, telling me a grizzly bear had entered the corral a hundred yards from his house and killed a ewe and two lambs. I arrived at the ranch two hours later and met Dave, the Montana Fish, Wildlife and Parks bear specialist.

The bite marks and hemorrhage we found after skinning the ewe confirmed they were bear kills, and now I needed to figure out how to catch them. Wayvan kept two guard dogs with his sheep, and two hound dogs ran free at the ranch. Those dogs made it difficult to set up equipment. Hanging the hindquarters of a sheep in a culvert trap or setting a conventional foot snare wouldn't work with all the dogs running around. However, the pipe snare set might. That setup was initially created by an Animal Damage Control (ADC) trapper in the 1960s. My district supervisor and I made some improvements and proved it worked. When done right, there were no worries about catching a dog. This would be the perfect place to give it a try.

The set was made using a six-inch-by-twelve-inch-long PVC pipe vertically placed in a hole, the top flush with the ground. A spring-powered throw-arm was put alongside the pipe with its trigger recessed seven inches deep and curved into the pipe through a slot on the side. A cable loop, whose tail was hooked to the throw-arm, was encircled around the top of the tube. Bait, such as sardines or meat, was placed at the bottom. A large rock then covered the pipe, making it dog-proof. After the bear rolled the rock off and reached for the bait, the

An armed pipe set

trigger deployed the upward thrust of the throw-arm, wrapping the cable loop tightly around its wrist. I caught most of my livestock-killing bears through the years with this method.

I next asked Wayvan to bring the loader tractor. We set the dead ewe into the bucket and placed her ten feet high atop an old chicken coop roof at the corral entrance. Below the sheep, I positioned a pipe in the ground at the corner of the building. The snare cable was then chained to a large, four-hundred-pound iron wheel to be used as an anchor.

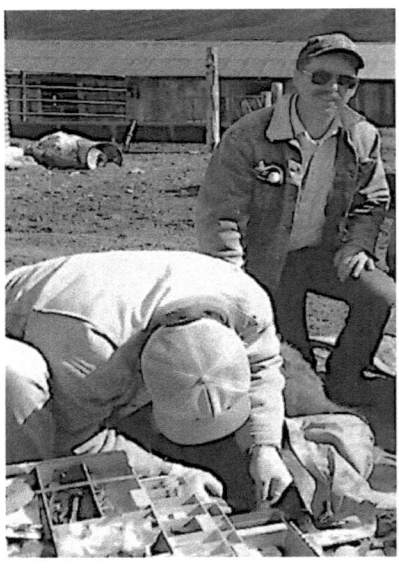

Taking tooth sample from the captured grizzly

Wayvan and Dave sat on the pickup's tailgate, visiting and watching me work. When finished, I felt confident we'd have a bear in the morning.

Early the following day, Wayvan called, saying we had caught the bear. I drove the fifty miles to the trap site as fast as possible, but not near as fast as the ten neighbors whom I found waiting there for me.

Driving down the ranch's steep road, I could see the bear. A medium-sized grizzly lying peacefully in the shade alongside the building, tired from being caught most of the night. I then noticed blood on the side of the chicken coop below an open window that had previously been covered. Oh, great! No matter how careful I was, there was always that one little thing I might overlook.

That little thing was a small shard of glass hidden in the wire-covered window that now protruded from the bear's neck. I had not only missed seeing it in the empty window, but my two partners sitting on the tailgate watching me had also not noticed it. To make matters worse, an audience watched our every move.

Our catch was a two or three-year-old sub-adult male in excellent shape. After judging its weight, Dave prepared a dart.

Dave's drug of choice at that time was Telazol, a safe dependable drug with a long recovery time. The mixture was drawn into a syringe and transferred into the dart. A small rubber stopper was slid over the needle's tip. Air was compressed into the other end of the dart. The dart was loaded into the barrel of the gun and a powder charge was inserted behind it. Once fired at the bear, the penetrating needle slipped the rubber collar allowing the tranquilizing drug to be released.

I kept the crowd back and covered Dave with the shotgun while the darting took place. After the bear was asleep, we studied the blood on the building; it wasn't as bad as we had initially thought. While removing the piece of glass with pliers, I heard a soft voice behind me say, "I could help here!" It was the husband of the neighbor's daughter. They were visiting from Washington state, and he happened to be an eye surgeon.

Dave always had a needle and thread in his kit, and without hesitation, the doctor went to work skillfully sewing closed the one-inch gash along the bear's neck. All the while, his wife took pictures.

The rest was routine: we put a plastic ID tag in the bear's ear, took measurements, and placed a radio telemetry collar around his neck. This collar emitted a specific signal that would enable us to track him. Lastly, we loaded the young male bear into a culvert trap for relocation since this was his first offense.

Captured bear resting alongside chicken coop

While we were discussing resetting the snare for the possibility of a second bear being involved, someone said, "Look there!" Five hundred yards away was another grizzly ambling down the open hillside in our direction, an unexpected sight at nine in the morning. This was likely the companion of the one we had just captured. The bear seemed oblivious to the ten people standing there. I quickly grabbed my shotgun, watched, and waited. At one hundred yards, the bear turned east and walked away.

Peering through the binoculars, Dave made out a familiar ear tag. That young male had previously been captured by MFWP in our area on a nuisance complaint and transferred to the west side of the Continental Divide. Two months later, it was grazing on grass near the Costco parking lot in Kalispell. MFWP free-darted the bear, and they returned the favor by relocating it back to our side.

Dave excitedly ran over to me and exclaimed, "That bear's got to go!" I agreed, not only because the bear had no fear of people, but because I felt he had something to do with this depredation. Wondering what to do next, Dave asked if we could use my agency pickup.

"Why?" I asked.

"If you drive, I'll get in the back with a dart gun and try to tranquilize the bear."

Whatever we decided, we had to do it fast as we watched the bear steadily lumber away.

My new pickup only had twelve hundred miles, and I wasn't excited about chasing a bear with it. Reluctantly, I jumped into the back and hurriedly rearranged things—then I had an idea. I told Dave that Wayvan had a four-wheeler that would be more maneuverable than darting from a pickup. The plan was changed, and in no time, Dave and his assistant Joe were on the four-wheeler, and Wayvan and I were in my pickup.

My shotgun was by my side in case things went sideways. The bear entered the meadow and slowly walked away, oblivious to our approach. There hadn't been any rain for most of the summer, so the land was dry.

As we drove toward the bear, it suddenly saw us and ran. The meadow was rough, and I was glad my equipment was secured in the back. Soon, the bear was directly in front of us.

Wayvan and I were on the left side, the four-wheeler was racing in on the right, and the bear in between. Dave raised his tranquilizer gun and, at twenty feet, made an impressive shot, placing the dart in the middle of the hind quarters.

Once darted, the bear kept running while we stopped. The meadow before us held no trees or willows, enabling us to watch the bear. He soon began to slow and then fell over, fast asleep. To my knowledge, that was the only grizzly bear ever darted from the back of a four-wheeler.

Our help arrived with a second culvert trap, and soon, the bear was loaded and on his way to town. After several phone calls that afternoon, the bear, unafraid of people, found his perfect home at the Chicago Zoo. The other bear I captured that day was relocated and was never heard from again.

Two days passed, and the Choteau paper ran a headline capturing everyone's attention: VISITING EYE DOCTOR DOES DOUBLE DUTY AS VET. The neighbor's daughter had taken her photos and shared the event with the newspaper. It was an amusing article about a bear barging through a chicken coop window. However, if that shard of glass had been a mere two inches lower, this lighthearted story would have had a very different ending, and it was a lesson I would never forget.

Mike with the livestock-killing bear after its capture

CHAPTER 9

A Strange Cup of Tea

"You prepare for every risk in the wild, but some dangers come from the least likely of places."

In the spring of 1995, I received a call that coyotes were killing lambs. The farm was owned by an elderly couple, Charles and Eva, and their thirty-year-old son, Fred. They seldom called regarding coyote trouble, as they had two good guard dogs that usually did their job. However, sometimes, even with the best preventive measures, the coyotes would still find ways to kill. The family asked if I could set up equipment for a short time to catch the coyotes causing the problem. They would tie up the guard dogs while the operation took place.

I arrived at the ancient two-story farmhouse on a blustery March day. Fred greeted me at the door, where we discussed the best way to do this before I drove to the kill site. The weather was bitter cold with a strong north wind. Even with gloves on, my hands were like ice as I finished my work. Fred drove out as I loaded the last of my equipment and kindly invited me in for coffee. I was chilled to the bone and more than welcomed the offer to go into the warm house and have something hot to drink.

It was an old farmhouse, and the floor creaked beneath my feet. As I walked into the warm kitchen, Fred's parents greeted me, happy for my help. They were in their eighties, and it was clear that they had their son Fred late in life. I sat at the wooden dining room table, where Fred brought us a steaming cup of hot water. He then offered tea, cocoa, and instant coffee. A hot cup of tea sounded good, so I put a Lipton tea bag in my cup of hot water.

I thoroughly enjoyed visiting with Charles. He was fun to listen to. Even at eighty years old, his mind was sharp. We talked about many things, including sheep, coyotes, and their way of life. His wife, Eva, was quieter but just as friendly.

After visiting for a while, I reached for my teacup and took a sip.

Oh my God!

The liquid burned its way down my throat, and not just because it was hot. It had a terrible taste, and I knew instantly something wasn't right. I could usually eat or drink almost anything to be polite, but there was no way this time! I didn't know these people well and felt embarrassed to say anything. One thing I did know, I wasn't going to drink another drop.

After a moment, Charles raised his cup and took a drink. The expression on his face changed, and he started coughing. "Fred!" he shouted between coughs. "Where did you get this water?"

Fred replied, "From the teakettle on top of the pellet stove.

"Oh no!" Charles exclaimed. "That water is for humidity and is full of Lime-A-Way. It's poison!"

At that moment, I just looked at him and was at a loss for words. After a minute of silence, I then confessed that when I had taken a drink earlier, it had tasted terrible. They all stared at me as if to say, "Why didn't you say something?"

All was quiet as Charles studied me, probably waiting to see if I was about to keel over. "I'm old," he said after a moment. "It's no big deal if I die, but I feel sorry for you." After sitting there a few minutes without any symptoms, I began to think maybe I hadn't been poisoned after all.

There was a somber atmosphere around the long table. Attempting to lighten the mood, I jokingly said, "Hey, I'm starting to get a little buzz. Can I have one more cup before I go?"

Everyone had a good laugh, and we relaxed and carried on our conversation. However, I couldn't help but wonder throughout the rest of that day just how much Lime-A-Way it would take to kill a person.

CHAPTER 10

Rancher Vows to Kill Grizzly

"Looking at the dead sheep lying in his field, the rancher's fury was waiting to explode."

People have mixed feelings regarding wolves, coyotes, mountain lions, and grizzly bears. Some want to save them all, while others wish them dead.

John, a sheepman in his fifties whose family had been on his ranch for over a hundred years, had no tolerance for grizzly bears. He grew up in a time when the thought of a grizzly grabbing sheep was absurd. A grizzly bear seldom ventured to the low country in the early days. If it did, it didn't last long. Now though, he worried every night. He used a llama and a guard dog, but those two deterrents had little effect on some bears.

One summer, on John's ranch a few miles from Choteau, Montana, I ran a snare line on the sheep pasture's south fence. If a coyote attempted to crawl under the fence to get to the sheep, the snares usually stopped them. I helped with the coyote predation. However, John didn't believe bears had any right to be on his land and, up until then, hadn't called me for help if one showed up to cause problems.

Checking snares one morning, I discovered an old ewe that had died of natural causes. In the past, I asked John to pick up his dead sheep and take them far away since they would attract bears. But no, he felt these bears shouldn't be there and wouldn't go out of his way to pick up the carcasses. I knew the dead sheep would be a problem; I should have picked it up myself that day, but in a hurry, I didn't.

On my next trip to check the snares, I noticed the sheep fence bent down where a bear had entered the pasture. The ewe I had found earlier was gone, and only a few tufts of wool remained.

When a bear became accustomed to eating dead sheep, it often started killing live ones. I worried that would be the case and wasn't surprised when I got the call less than a week later. Four ewes had been killed.

When I arrived, John angrily told me bear snares would not be set and he would accept nothing less than to see the bear shot. However, that was not how things were done back then. Unable to set snares, I offered to remove the dead sheep, to which he adamantly declined. There was nothing more I could do, so I left, knowing the bear would return, and wondered why he had even called me in the first place.

Over the next few days, several more sheep were killed. John called, and after a long conversation, I persuaded him to let me set snares. We both knew the killing would not stop now. John reluctantly agreed with the stipulation that Montana Fish, Wildlife, and Parks (FWP) would not be allowed on his property.

Several years before, our agency Wildlife Services (WS) signed an agreement with FWP to co-investigate when a grizzly was involved with livestock depredation. If we determined, in fact, that a bear had killed the animal, I did all the trapping. After catching the bear, I'd work with the FWP bear specialist to tranquilize, tag, and radio-collar the animal. The next step was to call the federal United States Fish and Wildlife (USFW) grizzly coordinator to determine the bear's fate: relocation or removal.

I explained to John that if we caught this bear, I would need the help of Dave, the FWP bear specialist. It would be difficult for one person to handle a bear. Also, it was strict protocol to have two people present when processing grizzlies for safety reasons. John finally agreed, but Dave could be there only *after* the capture. He was reluctant to grant this permission as FWP had been banned from his ranch years before due to a prior altercation.

That same day, a neighboring Hutterite colony informed me that a grizzly had killed seven ewes the previous night. It had fed on two of them, leaving the others untouched. The killing occurred in a big open field east of the highway, just a couple of miles from John's. I knew by the tracks it was the same bear.

After examining the kill site, I dragged all the dead sheep to a central location where one carcass had been fed upon more than the others. Afterward, I loaded all but that one sheep into my pickup. I then surrounded the ewe with a four-foot-high pen made of wood lath snow fence, leaving a three-foot opening on one end that narrowed at the bottom; there, I set a foot snare.

The trap was made by digging a twelve-inch-diameter hole about ten inches deep. A spring-powered throw-arm was placed alongside the hole. The throwing arm was depressed toward the pit, latching into a ten-inch-long trigger. The trigger extended over the depression and was supported by wooden sticks. A canvas covered the hole, and dirt was scattered on top to conceal the trap.

A snare cable was laid over the throw-arm, and a fourteen-inch loop was placed to surround the covered pit. When a bear stepped in the middle of the loop, the throwing arm would jerk upward, cinching the snare around the bear's wrist. The sheep were to stay in the pasture, but I felt confident the bear would return to the kill site that night and be caught.

Grizzly kills and a pen set at the neighboring Hutterite Colony

My supervisor, Frank, arrived that evening from Helena to accompany me in the morning. I was scheduled to attend a meeting in Denver the next day, and my plane departed late morning. We would have plenty of time to check and, if caught, process the bear. Many sheep had already been killed on the two ranches, and I wanted to see this finished, especially with the boss being there.

We turned off the highway early the next morning to check the snare. From a distance, I could see the still-standing snow fence and no bear. I was disappointed as I wanted to see this resolved before I left. My biggest disappointment, however, was yet to come.

Driving up to the set, we discovered that the bear *had* returned. My snare was sprung, and the sheep in the snow fence had been fed on. To make matters worse, looking to the east, were the remains of six more ewes freshly killed five hundred yards away. Frank was not impressed.

Radio, newspaper, and TV coverage had already taken place. In fact, two days earlier, *Great Falls Tribune* had printed a cover story featuring a large picture of John standing among several dead sheep.

The headline read: "Rancher Vows to Kill Grizzly."

I was sure that after this morning, the following story would be "Trapper Misses Capturing Killer Bear." Within hours, everyone in the country would know what had happened last night; there were no secrets in bear trapping.

I couldn't determine what went wrong. I reset the snare and caught my arm three times; it worked perfectly. Frank then commented, "Well, you did *something* wrong." He then urged me to catch my plane and said he would reset the snare and take care of the mess. Seeing how the bear had fed on the carcass, I felt it would return if Frank removed the six fresh kills and the remaining sheep were taken from the pasture.

With a sick stomach and the serious thought of changing careers, I drove to Great Falls to catch my plane. I had been looking forward to this trip for quite some time as our agency had planned a "Futuring Meeting" to discuss the program's course.

Several Wildlife Services state and regional directors, along with district supervisors from across the country, would attend, but only two field people in the United States had been invited. I happened to be one of them. That morning's experience was depressing, taking all the excitement out of my upcoming trip.

I arrived in Denver and went to the motel. I didn't sleep well that night. The following morning, my phone rang; it was Frank.

"Guess what?" he asked. Before I could reply, he said, "I missed him too!"

"What?"

"Yeah, the snare was sprung, but it didn't eat on the carcass this time. The bear was probably hit by the throw-arm when the snare fired. Now it'll never come back!"

I was secretly thrilled to hear this news. Not only would I get another chance at this bear, but if Frank had caught it, I would never have been able to live it down.

Frank reset the snare, but as we thought, the bear did not return. I couldn't wait to get home. The news of the bear lightened my mood, and I enjoyed the meeting after all.

It didn't take long after I returned home for the slaughter to continue. Behind John's house, another ewe was killed in a little grove of trees. It was a good place for a pen set, but I knew the bear was now wise to that trap.

It was time to get tricky.

I left the remains of the rumen (stomach) in place and dragged the carcass forty feet down a trail that ran through a stand of trees. Halfway down the trail, on one side of a fallen log that crossed the path, I constructed a blind snare set and made it look like nothing was there. A smaller log was placed on the other side with the loop of the foot snare in between.

I had just finished making the set when John brought word that a different Hutterite colony (twenty miles away) had a bear or bears come into their sheep corral and kill two ewes. The thought in the back of my mind about being grossly underpaid was suddenly remembered.

I headed in that direction and arrived late in the day. Setting the snares was a lot of work, but with the Hutterites' help, we constructed a couple of sets at the kill site before dark. Because we were worried about catching dogs from the colony, we set up a culvert trap that a bear could walk into to pull at a hanging sheep leg that would close the door behind it. We also placed a dog-proof pipe snare set covered with a large rock that only a bear could roll off before reaching into the pipe to be caught.

At daylight the following day, I got a call from the colony informing me that a bear had been captured in the pipe. John would check the snares at his place, so I wasn't worried about them.

The sheep-killing grizzly finally captured

I arrived at the colony and met Dave from FWP. We had tranquilized the bear and started to process it when a colony member drove up and told me I needed to call home. It must be important as they knew I had caught a bear and was busy. There were no cell phones then, so I had to go to the boss' house, the only phone allowed in the colony of one hundred people.

I called home and was informed that I needed to phone John right away. They didn't know why, but I figured it had something to do with my snares. I called John.

When he picked up, there were no greetings. All he said was, "I'm looking out my window at that sheep-killing bear in your snare. Now you, myself, and my wife are the only ones who know about this, so if I shoot it, will you turn me in?"

Talk about being between a rock and a hard spot.

I knew the bear needed to be removed, but this wasn't the way to do it. I talked for ten minutes, trying to convince him not to shoot the bear. With the number of sheep killed, I felt sure the USFW, who had the final say, would do what was right. However, I was unsure if I had successfully talked John into not killing it. I hung up, and we hurriedly finished with bear number one.

When we arrived at John's, I didn't know if the bear would be dead or alive. Driving to the set, I saw the bear standing there; it felt like the world's weight had been lifted off my shoulders. For many days, in the media and the coffee shops, the whole episode had been quite the topic of conversation, and now it would soon be over.

She was a three-year-old sub-adult. Young bears were often a large part of my workload as they were like teenagers and prone to get in trouble. At that time, sow grizzlies were allowed three strikes before they were removed from the population. The carnage this bear had inflicted should have counted as ten strikes, but that was not the case. Since it was her first capture, USFW decided to move her as far away as possible and give her one last chance. That wasn't right after all we'd just gone through. However, I had no say in the matter.

In the middle of processing the bear, John drove up. He and his wife took pictures and were unhappy to see Dave there. They became even more upset when they learned the bear was getting another chance. I told John that after it was released, and if she caused trouble again, the situation would attract a lot of attention and help his cause. Without a word, John stared at me, put his pickup in gear, and sped off.

We collared the bear and attached an oversized white ear tag with an X. This would help identify her later. With a happy heart, I pulled my equipment that day. What an ordeal and an education that had been. To say I was glad it was over was an understatement.

The bear was relocated to the west side of the Continental Divide, roughly eighty-five air miles away. Within a few days, a calf was killed and bitten on top of the nose, a trademark of this particular bear. The radio collar was a big help in locating her at the kill site. The signal allowed the agencies to find and shoot the grizzly, so all the work and anguish I had experienced was not in vain. That bear was one of the worst livestock killers I had ever seen. In the aftermath, many other sheep carcasses were discovered. The exact number of sheep she killed will never be known.

It's fortunate that only a small percentage of predators, whether they are bears, lions, wolves, or coyotes, have the tendency to kill livestock. Once they start, they often will continue and need to be dealt with.

"So why didn't you let me kill her that day?" John asked me a few months later.

I glanced at him. "At the time, I thought the other agencies would do the right thing. But I was wrong."

John grumbled in response.

"You've got your ranch and money in the bank. Had you been caught and been forced to pay the fine, it wouldn't have been a problem. But me?" I chuckled. "I have two small kids, no money in the bank, *and* I happen to like my job, a job I would be without if I had been caught up in the middle of something like that."

Through the years, I learned how things worked. People like John, who tell everyone what they're going to do, even putting their picture in the paper under the headline "Rancher Vows to Kill Grizzly," were not the bear killers. The real bear killers, I came to realize, never said a word.

CHAPTER 11

Do You Smell Something Dead at Castle Reef?

"The claws on the fence told the story, but it was the lion in the shadows that made it unforgettable."

Gary, the game warden in Augusta, called late one afternoon to inform me that a mountain lion had killed an elk. Initially, I thought, *Isn't that what they're supposed to do?*

No, not in this case. Mountain lions were *not* supposed to be killing domestic elk confined in a forty-acre pasture and worth big money. During that time, farm-raised elk were a fad, sold for meat, similar to ostriches. The rancher was a breeder, and his female elk calves were contracted to sell that fall at

$4,000 each and the male calves at $2,500. Losing the calf was a significant loss. Confined elk were considered livestock, so that was the reason I was called.

I packed my equipment and drove fast to cover the one hundred miles to the ranch and hoped to have enough daylight left to do something once I arrived. The ranch was nestled in the pines at the base of a mountainfront. Above it was a large rock wall known as Castle Reef.

When I arrived, Rick, the owner, his friend Fred, and Gary were waiting for me. They had removed the elk herd from the pasture, leaving it empty upon my arrival. And what a pasture it was. A small creek flowed through the center; thick brush, willows, and pines lined the banks. A twelve-foot chain-link fence surrounded the forty-acre enclosure with telephone poles used as posts. It was quite a setup and must have been costly to build.

We made our way to the creek where Rick led us to the remains of a half-grown elk calf lying in shallow water; it was partially eaten and surrounded by lion tracks in the mud. It was a male: $2,500 instead of $4,000. It could have been worse.

It was late, and with little time to spare, I quickly walked down the creek, finding more lion tracks. Twenty yards from the kill site, Rick and Gary were talking.

As I approached, Gary asked, "Do you smell something dead?"

I said, "Yes," and we soon discovered the source—another dead calf was hidden behind a tall pine tree. A female, this time worth $4,000. The calf had been killed two days prior and was freshly fed upon. This looked like an ideal spot for a foot snare, but we were running out of daylight.

By now, Rick was visibly upset. Without saying a word, he turned away in disgust and walked toward his house, a half mile away. Gary and I returned to my pickup to gather the snares, leaving Fred behind at the kill site. On the way, I told Gary, "I'll bet that lion is still in the pasture." Lions were so reclusive and often watched from the shadows.

We were returning with the snares when we heard a shot.

It was Fred.

Forty yards from the kill, he had surprised the lion that had been lying there watching us the whole time. He shot at it with his .38 pistol and thought it might be hit but wasn't sure. I ran to the pickup for my guns. I then handed Gary the 220 Swift rifle and kept the Benelli 12 gauge loaded with copper BBs for myself.

I then told them, "With the tall enclosure, the lion's probably still here."

It was three hundred yards downstream to the east fence, and I slowly walked in that direction along the north side of the brushy creek. Gary and Fred were on the south side, and it was getting dark.

At first, the foliage was open, and we could keep track of each other. But the brush grew thicker as we proceeded, and finally, I couldn't see them at all. I went slow, peering intently into the trees in case the lion had climbed one. Then, before me, I spotted the faint outline of the east fence in the fading light. I stopped, wondering what to do next.

"There it is!" shattered the silence.

A gunshot followed.

Moments later, another shot rang out. This time, I heard the bullet whizz by in front of me, dangerously close. Two thoughts raced through my mind: the lion must be coming toward me and I hope I don't get shot. Then, like a ghost appearing out of thin air, the lion emerged from the thick brush ten yards ahead of me, loping north. In the dim light, it was running fast and taking long strides. I raised my shotgun, fired, and watched as the lion tumbled to the ground.

It was a young male, around two years old. With ninety pounds of pure muscle, it was easy to see how he could kill one of the calves. I was glad it was over; better yet, I didn't have to set snares in the dark.

When we arrived at the house that evening, we found the rancher elated. Much different from when I last saw him. I asked if I could use his phone to call home. He said, "You can do anything you like on my ranch tonight." After saying goodbye, I gave the lion to Gary and headed the one hundred miles back home.

The following day, while Rick was installing an electric wire along the top of the enclosure to prevent further loss, he discovered claw marks on the telephone poles, revealing exactly how the lion had managed to get over the tall fence.

Two days later, just when I started to think my summer would finally slow down, I received yet another call from Rick. He said that evening, driving into the yard, he had seen another lion west of the house chasing his horses. There evidently had been more than one.

I returned to the ranch early the next day, and we looked over the horse pasture. This would be difficult as I had no kill to set on. I knew if the lion wasn't captured, there would be an excellent chance it would kill one of the small colts or perhaps find another way into the elk pasture. We located two good spots outside the fence where I set foot snares, one on each side of the pasture.

The setup was the same as the bear snare but with a smaller 5/32-inch cable. A spring-powered throw arm was attached to the snare loop, which would cinch around the lion's leg if it stepped within the circle. For bait, I used sardines. I hung a cotton ball on a string from a nearby branch as a visual attractant. Cats had terrific eyesight. Combined with their curiosity, the cotton ball was the perfect lure.

When my sets were finished, Rick looked at me and shook his head. "Sardines and a cotton ball! Do you honestly believe that will work?"

I replied, "Nothing is certain, but now, at least, we have a chance, even if it's a slim one."

The following day, my phone rang, and it was Rick. "You got the lion; that snare actually worked!"

It turned out to be an older female, over a hundred pounds, and most likely the mother of the young male I had shot earlier.

First impressions, good or bad, have a lasting impact. I had only worked in my district for a short time when that occurred, and I hoped to stay there for the remainder of my life.

Success goes a long way, but stories of failure travel farther.

Little did I know, driving home that summer night so many years ago, I would spend the rest of my career in Montana and of all the adventures that lay ahead.

CHAPTER 12

The Bawling Bear

"In the wild, waiting is the hardest part—especially when there is the promise of company you don't want to meet."

As the sun rose on a quiet Saturday morning, I sat in my pickup west of Dupuyer, Montana, watching a large sow grizzly captured in my foot snare. It was amazing how much of my bear work occurred on the weekends and holidays. Coyote work could wait until Monday, but that was not the case with wolves and grizzlies, where capturing them the first night was my best chance for success.

The dead calf had been discovered the previous day, and after confirming it was killed by a bear, I set a foot snare at the entrance of a pen made of logs stacked around the carcass.

It paid off.

We found no tracks on our investigation, so were unsure what kind of bear or bears we were dealing with. Using my newly acquired cell phone, I called my co-worker Dave to tell him a bear had been captured.

As I sat in my pickup, waiting for Dave to arrive, I looked up in time to watch two yearling grizzly cubs emerge from the brush patch where the sow was captured. They hurriedly ran one hundred yards uphill and disappeared into a grove of chokecherries. I was happy my snare had worked and was even more grateful the sow was captured instead of one of her cubs, which would have complicated things.

A couple of hours later, Dave showed up. The first part was routine. We drove in close and darted the sow; it was her first capture, so she was radio-collared, measured, and tagged before being placed into a culvert trap. Now, what were we going to do about the cubs?

After some discussion, we loaded tranquilizer into three darts. Carrying our two dart guns, with one dart to spare, we made our way into the chokecherry patch to attempt free-darting one or both of the cubs. We were not completely sure these were the bears responsible for the kill, but if successful, we desired to relocate the family group just to be safe.

I brought with me a .44 Magnum pistol. I wasn't very confident with my pistol shooting ability, but if nothing else, the big noise it made might scare things away. My shotgun would have been a much better option but carrying the dart gun made that impossible. This was before we started using bear spray, so the pistol was my only choice. The sow was in the culvert, and these were just yearlings. I wasn't worried at the time, but all that was about to change.

We cautiously made our way into the dense bushes. It was a tangled, dark place and difficult to see. Suddenly, the bears jumped from their beds ten yards away. I aimed at the one on the right, and Dave took aim at the bear on the left. Shooting through foliage was difficult as the darts could be easily deflected. The bears were close and running broadside away from us, branches breaking in their path. We both fired, and a cub let out a growl, suggesting at least one dart had struck its target. We watched the bears exit the chokecherries and run over the ridge.

We followed to see where they went before entering the dense trees on the other side, but it was too late. Standing atop the ridge, we looked down into the deep, broad canyon of aspens and willows that stretched below us and wondered where they had gone.

Dave carried the remaining dart gun as we walked through the thick trees. It was a jungle, and our chances of finding the tranquilized bear or its partner were slim. I went to the west while Dave headed east.

After walking a couple hundred yards, the silence was broken by branches snapping and something running ahead of me through the thick trees. A deer? A bear? I could see movement through the shaded aspens but couldn't tell what it was.

I slowed, wishing now more than ever that I had my shotgun instead of the pistol. Then, I heard growls and saw the bushes moving right before me. A bear's head emerged from the foliage not thirty yards away, appearing much larger than it actually was.

I pulled my pistol, ready to shoot, before realizing it was one of the yearlings, not entirely under the effects of whatever tranquilizer it had received. The bear was lively and thrashed around but had lost its ability to run. I called out for Dave, who was close by. He had heard the bear and was already heading in my direction.

After he arrived, we discussed our options, and he handed me the dart gun. I'd wait there while Dave returned to his pickup for more drugs. We hoped I would get the chance to tranquilize the sibling with our last dart, should it appear.

The aspens, where the cub was located, were dense and spindly, making them impossible for me to climb. Unfortunately, there were no larger trees nearby. Climbing one would have been safer and allowed me much better visibility.

Years before, someone had cleared a wide path to build a fence through these trees. The bear lay on the edge of this opening. I planned to wait at the base of the trees, twenty yards from the bear on the opposite edge.

I sat, and after a while, the bear before me started bawling. It was the high-pitched bawl of a young bear in distress calling for its mother. *All right, this should bring that other bear in*, I thought. Then, the bawling grew louder.

There were only a handful of days on the Rocky Mountain Front when the wind didn't blow, and this was one of them. As I listened to the cub's cries, I thought about the pup-in-distress calls for coyotes that I sometimes used—and started getting nervous.

Older coyotes would often come running in with their hair raised and teeth barred, ready to defend their young when they heard such a cry. What was happening now was precisely like that, except this time, it was a bear-in-distress call.

I'm not ashamed to admit that I instantly went from nervous to frightened. With no wind, I was sure that even though this bear's mother was in the culvert, any other grizzly within two miles would hear the cub's cries and come running. I held my pistol tight, but if a bear suddenly charged in like some coyotes I had seen, the chance to stop it at close range with my lackluster pistol-shooting ability was slim. The urge to get up and run grew stronger with every passing second.

It was only a half hour before I heard Dave's pickup approaching, but it was the *longest* half-hour I had ever spent.

We knew the bear required more drugs; the best method to administer them under the circumstances was through a jab stick. The tool consisted of a five- or six-foot-long pipe made of metal or plastic, with a syringe attached to one end and a push-button rod on the other. When possible, the drug could be safely administered to an animal by this method and was gentler on them than the dart gun.

Slowly and carefully, Dave approached the bear, waiting until the animal stopped struggling, then quickly injected the drug. Within minutes, the cub was unconscious. We then loaded it in the pickup and drove to the culvert to lay it alongside its mother, still under sedation. After transporting them to where we tranquilized the yearling, we set another culvert trap alongside, hoping the remaining cub would return and be captured.

The next morning, I was optimistic about our chance of success. But, when we arrived, the sliding door of the culvert was still open. We then faced a difficult decision: release the two bears on-site, hoping they'd reunite with the remaining cub, or try to relocate the sow and captured cub. We chose the first option. Many cattle were still in the pasture, but we were not sure these bears were responsible for killing the calf. If the sow and cub were hauled away, there was a good chance the second cub wouldn't make it alone.

That day, I had the rare opportunity to bring my young son and daughter along to release the bears. The protocol was much more relaxed back then. It was a once-in-a-lifetime experience for them since bear calls were seldom safe enough to take other people. That day was an exception since they could watch from the pickup. Besides, it was a Sunday.

Chad and Katie peering at the captured bears within the culvert trap

We named the yearling female cub after my daughter, Katie. Some people didn't like the practice of naming bears, but it was so much easier to remember than numbers. Overall, it was an unforgettable experience for both Katie and my son Chad.

Years later, as I write this, I am grateful that my daughter didn't cause the trouble Katie the Bear ended up causing! But that's a story for another time.

A Night With The Chicken Lady

CHAPTER 13

A Night with the Chicken Lady

"On a day the world stood still, I found myself in a place time had forgotten, sharing an unforgettable night with the Chicken Lady."

On the afternoon of September 10, 2001, I received a call that grizzly bears had attacked and killed several sheep seventy-five miles away. It had already been a long day, and this news meant it was about to get longer. I gathered my bear equipment and headed toward the location.

The ranch was a rundown place I'd never been to before. An elderly woman approaching eighty greeted me. She owned the small flock of sheep the bear had attacked and was extremely happy I was there. Her husband had passed away years before, and not wanting to leave her home, she had chosen to stay. Besides the sheep, her only company was an old border collie. It looked like she led a very lonely life.

The old farmstead sat in a coulee bottom, surrounded by gnarled cottonwood trees. The location was on the open prairie, where trees were scarce, twenty miles from the mountainfront, and not ideal bear habitat by any means. The house was at least one hundred years old and resembled the derelict outbuildings and corrals alongside it.

There was nothing fancy about the woman. She was not tall, but she was a little on the heavy side. Her face showed years of hard work. The old woman guided me toward the corrals where the killing occurred.

While I was examining the kills, Dave arrived, and upon further investigation, we discovered where a sow grizzly and two yearling cubs had entered the corral and killed three sheep. All were fed on, but much remained. If this had happened closer to thick trees and vegetation, I'd have bet the bears were nearby. However, as open as this was with nowhere to hide, they had likely moved on and would not return. I grabbed snares from my pickup in case I was wrong.

Typical grizzly feeding pattern

As I was setting the snares, the woman grew visibly upset. She was not only convinced the bears would return but that they would also come into her house that night and kill her. Despite living in the area for most of her life, she had little experience with bears. I tried to tell her she would be safe if she stayed in the house until I returned early the next morning. It was obvious by the expression on her face that she doubted my words.

Grizzly tracks

By the time I finished setting the snares, it was late. The old woman approached me and, with a worried voice, asked, "Could you please stay here tonight? I have an extra bed, and supper is ready." It was already 9 p.m., and I was hungry. I hadn't eaten since lunch and needed to be back early to check the snares. The thought of a meal and saving myself a one-hundred-fifty-mile roundtrip was tempting. Plus, I couldn't help feeling sorry for her, so I accepted the invitation.

After Dave and I entered the living room of the old house, I shared my plan with him. He suggested that if I was staying, I should bring a shotgun inside just in case.

As we discussed this, the old woman grabbed a pistol from the table beside the couch. She exclaimed, "I have a gun!" and waved the barrel in our direction.

In a panic, I told her, "Please put that thing away." I assured her my shotgun was all we needed. I always had a phobia about people pointing guns at me, especially this old woman who didn't seem to know one end of that pistol from the other. Afterward, she and I stood on the porch and watched Dave drive away. At that moment, I began to regret my decision to stay.

The dilapidated old house had seen better days. It had been neglected and was in need of a good cleaning. I had stayed in rough camps, but this was one of the roughest. The living room furniture was straight out of the 1940s and covered with dirty blankets. Enough dirt to plant a flower crowded every corner. The rest of the old house was the same.

However, I was committed now; there was no turning back.

It had been an incredibly long day. After we locked the sheep in the barn, I was tired and hungry, glad it was finally time to eat. "Chicken, baked potatoes, and store-bought macaroni salad!" she exclaimed. She told me she hated to cook and would buy several large boxes of frozen fried chicken. Occasionally, she'd bake a box with a bunch of potatoes. She ate the same meal every night, day after day, until it was gone, then made another batch.

Though she had no chickens, I jokingly named her (not to her face) the "Chicken Lady."

The latest batch on the counter looked like it had already been there for several days. The chicken was dried out and resembled jerky, but I was hungry, and it didn't matter. I did, however, have second thoughts about the macaroni salad, remembering all those food poisoning stories I'd heard. I ate it anyway.

As the long summer evening turned to night, the Chicken Lady told me, "You can sleep in my bed, and I'll take the couch."

She was eighty, and I didn't want to take her bed. "That's nice of you, but I'll sleep on the couch."

"No, I sleep better on the couch," she replied, moving to sit. "I sleep there most nights anyway."

I grabbed my shotgun and entered the bedroom, placing it in the corner beside the bed. The window alongside the bed faced the corrals where the sheep had been killed, forty yards away. The bedroom was as dirty as the rest of the house. Below the window were no fewer than a thousand dead flies on the filthy carpet. The sheets were dirty and hadn't been washed for quite some time.

Sitting on the edge of the bed, I looked around. The living room was definitely forties decor, but the bedroom was stuck in the 1930s.

After removing my shoes and socks as if it mattered, I brushed the dead flies off the bottom of my feet before getting into bed. Lying down, I immediately sank into a hole in the center.

No wonder my hostess preferred the couch!

The night felt like it would never end, and I hardly got any sleep. If any bears returned, I certainly would have heard them, but all was quiet.

When it was light enough to see, I dressed and grabbed my shotgun before heading out the door to check the snares. The Chicken Lady was still asleep on the couch when I left. Passing through the kitchen, I noticed the chicken and potatoes still sitting on the counter. However, the macaroni salad was missing, which was a relief.

I quietly slipped out the door in the early morning light. Despite the silence, I proceeded cautiously. The quiet didn't mean bears weren't around. I checked my snare lines but wasn't surprised to see them empty.

Upon returning to the house, I found my hostess had the TV on. She pointed to a news story about a plane that she explained had accidentally flown into one of the Twin Towers. It didn't look like an accident, and I wondered what was happening.

Before leaving, I informed her I'd keep my snares set two more nights in case the bears returned, and I'd be back in the morning. As I drove away, I heard on the radio that a second plane had also hit the second tower. I knew then it was no accident.

The bears never returned. While removing my snares a few days later, I gazed around, imagining what this once-beautiful ranch might have looked like. That day was the last time I saw the Chicken Lady or the ranch. I heard she continued living there for a couple more years.

But eventually, all things come to an end.

Anyone old enough at the time remembers precisely where they were when they first heard the news of the terrorist attacks on September 11, 2001. On that day, two memories were forever etched in my mind. The Twin Towers and my unforgettable night with the Chicken Lady.

CHAPTER 14

Everything Happens
for a Reason

"The course of life often hinges on events we never see coming. A single moment, the right place, the right time."

The year 2004 was hectic. It began on April 1 with a calf killed by a grizzly west of Choteau. I caught two bears at the kill site and then three others in bee yards. A total of five grizzlies in three days. At the same time, a mountain lion was killing lambs near Dupuyer, and of course, there was the never-ending coyote problem. However, that summer something unforgettable happened that helped me realize how certain events guided my life and how everything happens for a reason.

In June, another sow grizzly and two sub-adults were killing sheep near Choteau. The dead sheep were found in thick vegetation near the producer's house. After confirming the kills, I set three foot snares, confident the bears would return. However, to my disappointment, only one of the two-year-olds was captured the following morning.

Bears, once snared, make a lot of noise, especially cubs and sub-adults. The adults emit a deep growl while the cubs vocalize in higher pitches.

After the bear was caught that night, the rancher heard it from his house, a half mile away. It wasn't until two years later that I learned what happened that night.

When he heard the bear, the rancher woke his wife. Together, on his four-wheeler, they drove to the trap site in the dark. The snares were set in an opening surrounded by thick brush and willows. As they approached, illuminated in the lights of the four-wheeler, they spotted a sub-adult grizzly caught in a snare ten yards away. He told his wife, "This might not be a good place to be." Which was an understatement! The sow was surely close by, and the four-wheeler offered little protection.

They hurriedly turned around and drove back toward the house. This explained why I thought it strange when checking the snares at daylight to find only the sub-adult was caught, and my other two snares were still set. Driving in that night, the couple had scared off the other bears, ruining my chance to capture them.

The next morning, using telemetry, we located a radio-collared sow close by. This was another reason the bears had left; the mother bear was snare-wise. The signal came from the collar of a bear I had caught a couple of years before after it had destroyed a bee yard.

After tranquilizing, measuring, and collaring the two-year-old male, we placed him into a culvert trap. I set three well-hidden snares in the nearby trails surrounding the culvert, hoping the family group would return. However, the bears didn't come back, and we were later forced to pull the equipment and release the sub-adult on-site. To my disappointment, monitoring his radio collar verified that the young bear remained alone in the area close to the sheep.

Over the next few days, the rancher and FWP installed an electric fence around the sheep pasture to protect them from future depredation. Part of the fence, however, crossed swamp ground where vegetation grew high, which could cause the fence to short out. The fence shorting out would open the door for the bear to kill again. A short time later, that is precisely what happened.

Several more sheep were found dead in the corral and others in the pasture next to the rancher's house. The telemetry signal proved it was the work of the collared sub-adult. Besides liking mutton, this bear had little respect for humans and frequented the rancher's home. The producer was worried for his sheep and his children.

It was clear that something needed to be done.

Concerned about other sheep and families in the surrounding area, FWP and USFWS thought it was best to remove the bear. After the order was given, my supervisor, Greg, arrived to help.

Later that evening, we made our way up a wobbly ladder to the top of the barn. On one side, the barn had a flat roof that overlooked the corral and the meadow to the west. We had removed the sheep kills from the pasture, and hoped the grizzly would return to feed on the dead sheep in the corral from the previous night. Despite being summer, there was a chill in the air. We had brought a spotlight, a shotgun, a night-vision rifle, and, most importantly, our coats. We spent the time quietly visiting while we waited, listening for the signal from the telemetry receiver that would alert us of the bear's approach.

Greg was the supervisor for the west side of a vast state, and it was evident he was happy to be there that night. Being in the field was what he loved most and rarely had the chance to experience such days. At three in the morning, we heard the signal of the approaching bear's collar; it grew louder as the bear drew closer. That woke us up, and in anticipation, we waited to see what would happen next.

The meadow was open from the corral to the west for two hundred yards; beyond that were cottonwood trees and thick underbrush. The bear came to the edge of the trees and stopped, hidden in the dense willows and unable to be seen with night-vision equipment. We were hesitant to use the spotlight, which might scare him off. For five minutes, we anxiously waited, listening to the steady *beep-beep* of the telemetry, but he refused to emerge from the dense foliage into the meadow. How disappointing this was after waiting in the cold most of the night. As if he sensed our presence, the bear left, and the signal faded until he was gone.

We climbed down from the barn at daylight and loaded our equipment. The bear had headed south, so we pointed the pickup in that direction. The Teton River emerged east from the mountains north of Choteau, then curved and flowed south toward town. Using telemetry, we found the signal in the trees beside the river, five miles from where we had been waiting.

Homes were nearby, so we would have to postpone our plan and figure out what to do next.

While all this bear activity was happening, a coyote was killing lambs in the Sweet Grass Hills near the Canadian border. Trying to get this stopped, I set M-44s near the kills. Used primarily on private grounds, M-44s were single lethal-dose devices that featured a narrow six-inch tube that was driven into the earth, and a hollow one-inch-tall head with a small dose of cyanide screwed onto a plunger. The ejector was then placed into the tube. It triggered when a coyote grabbed the scented cloth-wrapped head, pulling it upward thereby discharging the cyanide. Death occurred suddenly and often targeted the coyote responsible for the kill. I usually had great success with these. M-44s were selective, so sheep and most other animals wouldn't bother them.

It was one of my few options, as I could not set traps or other equipment with the sheep nearby. Unfortunately, the M-44s hadn't worked this time as the coyote didn't like to return to previous kills, or if it did, it was uninterested. Coyotes generally took the biggest and fattest lambs, but this one differed. It always killed the smaller lambs, which I thought strange. I knew I needed to find a way to stop this, or the killing would continue all summer.

I called the office, requesting our helicopter, which was paid for in part by the producers. Typically, when it came, I would fly for two or three days at a time. Being responsible for livestock depredations in five counties, flying was a valuable tool and the only way I could keep up. Recently, our agency had acquired a newer Hughes 500 helicopter. We were fortunate to have Tim, an excellent pilot, who was busy installing equipment and preparing it for use.

When I called, Tim said at least a couple more days were needed before it would be ready. I had no other choice but to keep after the coyote on the ground. Options were limited; I tried calling by imitating the sounds of a wounded deer and a baby lamb, hoping to attract and shoot the coyote, but no luck. The country was open, windy, and difficult to sneak across. As the number of kills increased, all eyes watched to see if I could stop it.

In the sheep pasture early one morning, the wind was blowing as usual. I would attempt to call, check equipment, and count how many more lambs had been killed. Concealing my pickup in the bottom of a coulee, I walked a half mile to try calling. At the second calling location, the wind briefly died down. I couldn't see them but heard the blatting of sheep in a creek bottom south of me. Taking my rifle, I sneaked down a coulee with the wind in my favor. As I slipped over the dam of a little reservoir, I spotted sheep. They were bunched around a curve of the coulee, and I could see only part of the herd. The way they behaved made me think a coyote was close by.

After lying quietly on the dam for ten minutes, I saw the flock suddenly start to mill around, and a coyote magically appeared in the middle of them. It was one hundred fifty yards away, on a sidehill surrounded by sheep. *This* was the coyote I had been after. However, I hesitated to shoot, knowing that if I missed, I might kill a sheep.

The flock created a wider opening as the coyote prowled ahead; it paused, giving me my chance. The killing stopped with one squeeze of the trigger. She was a dry female, which helped explain why she killed the smaller lambs; there were no pups to feed.

Returning to the pickup, I felt good about what had happened. However, my happiness faded while listening to the new voicemail on my phone. The message was from Dave, saying the bear I had caught earlier had killed more sheep near Choteau.

When I phoned my supervisor, updating him on the latest bear trouble, he asked if I still needed the helicopter. I explained that I had just shot the lamb-killing coyote and suggested the chopper go elsewhere, as now I had this bear to deal with.

I returned Dave's call, and he told me the bear was bedded along an irrigation ditch north of Choteau. He thought we could use telemetry to locate the collar and approach within shotgun range. If successful, we could finish this.

I was one hundred twenty-five miles away and drove there as quickly as possible. Dave was waiting at the same sheep ranch where the bear had been captured. With telemetry, he had located the young grizzly, bedded in thick trees and willows.

After examining the latest kills, we drove to the site, turned on the telemetry, and anxiously walked toward the sleeping bear.

Each collared bear was assigned a different-numbered frequency. Utilizing telemetry, we scanned with a handheld antenna to determine the bear's location by the strength of the signal. The disadvantage was that we not only relied on the signal's strength for direction but for distance as well. The louder the signal the closer we were. This could be deceiving, as a bear, thought to be fifty yards away, could in reality be only ten yards. But one thing was certain: we were getting closer to a bear.

Unfortunately, the willows were so dense that it was nearly impossible to see more than five feet ahead, let alone five yards.

I possessed a focus that was hard to explain, and my heart pounded louder with each step.

Bears, like people, were different, depending on the circumstances. Most would run, but some would stand their ground. Sometimes, a wounded bear that would typically run would attack. Even a younger bear like this could be dangerous if it felt cornered.

The willows were so thick in places we had to crawl to get through them. Dave turned the volume of the signal down in his headphones as it grew louder. We knew then the bear was bedded right before us.

We were quiet and hoped to get as close as possible in this jungle before he sensed our presence. I raised my shotgun as the brush ahead shook and branches broke.

The bear jumped up and ran, invisible in the dense willows, and was gone. This was nerve-wracking, but what an indescribable feeling of excitement being that close to a bedded grizzly. Our only option now was to wait and try again tomorrow, hoping he'd be bedded in a better place.

The following day, Dave called to tell me he'd located the bear in a horseshoe-shaped patch of willows. The foliage wasn't as thick, and he thought it would be a better place than the previous day.

He was partially right. As we walked in, at first, it *was* a better place, but when we were within forty yards of the bedded bear, I told Dave I was afraid this would be the same as the day before. The closer we drew, the thicker the brush became. I was sure that once we got close enough and he knew we were there, the bear would escape precisely like before.

"What if I call and see if the helicopter is available?" I asked Dave. "This would be a perfect place to hover; it is open on three sides, and I could finish this when the bear ran out." Walking into thick willows to shoot bears was never one of my favorite parts of the job, and I thought this would be much safer.

Dave replied with a shrug, "Whatever you think will work."

After we silently backed away, I called the pilot, who informed me that George, the trapper to the south, had canceled that day, so he was available. Then, calls were made up the ladder to obtain permission to use the helicopter. Until now, to my knowledge, this was the first attempt to take a grizzly in the Lower Forty-Eight from the air. After permission was granted, Tim was on his way. It was only a thirty-minute flight, and the helicopter was there in no time.

The five-year-old Hughes 500 the agency had recently purchased had all the bells and whistles, quite an upgrade from our twenty-five-year-old helicopter. I loaded my equipment, figuring this wouldn't take long if things went according to plan. I couldn't wear a helmet that day because headphones were needed for the telemetry. Back then, the helmet's audio system was not coordinated with telemetry as it is now. I knew I was sticking my neck out by not wearing a helmet and felt naked without it, but it was the only way.

Tim and I took off in the helicopter while Dave drove the pickup toward the sleeping bear. In moments, we were hovering over the willows. The signal was strong above the trees; however, the foliage was so dense that the bear could not be seen. Then, suddenly, the telemetry indicated the grizzly was on the move. Tim held over the willows, and the bear emerged, running fast before us.

I threw the telemetry antenna in the back seat and reached for the shotgun. The bear was in the open but would not be for long as he headed toward the next willow patch. I knew I had to get him before he reached the willows and disappeared. As Tim closed in, using slugs, I took five shots as quickly as I could pull the trigger; I did not want this bear to get away or, worse yet, wound him.

It was over in a moment. The flight lasted only twelve minutes. After landing, we met Dave and loaded the bear into his pickup. It wasn't the largest bear, but he had caused a great number of problems.

I never enjoyed this part of the job but knew it had to be done; otherwise, the trouble would continue. Dave would take the bear to the state lab in Bozeman for analysis.

Before Tim departed, I thanked him and headed home, relieved this was finally finished. What a summer it had been. The coyote up north, the bear projects, and the mountain lion problem were finally over. I knew, however, that some other dilemma would be coming soon; it always did.

The next day, Tim flew south and met George, the trapper who had canceled. They were hunting only for a short time before the engine of the new helicopter suddenly quit. The aircraft came down abruptly; it bounced once on the right skid and then fell onto its right side, tearing off the main rotor and tail. The helicopter lay sideways where it stopped.

On the upper side, Tim asked George if he was okay, and he replied, "I think I have a broken leg."

Looking back, Tim saw flames coming from the engine. "Broken leg or not, we need to get out!" he exclaimed.

Tim helped George climb from the wreckage and turned off the fuel. They then climbed a safe distance up a nearby hillside and watched. The flames went out when the jet fuel in the line was consumed, preventing the helicopter from burning.

It turned out George didn't have a broken leg after all. He was severely bruised and had a nasty scrape. His helmet was cracked from the top down one side. The day before, that crack could have been on my head. The helmet had saved his life.

Later, we discovered the helicopter had crashed due to a faulty part, the same part responsible for two other crashes that year involving the Hughes 500. George was fortunate the accident happened where it had and to be flying with an experienced pilot like Tim. It could have been so much worse!

The moral of the story was that if I hadn't shot the lamb-killing coyote in the Sweet Grass Hills that day, because we usually flew two or three days at a time, I would have been flying and involved in a crash. We often flew over trees and mountainous terrain, so the accident could have happened in a far worse location. Thankfully, even though the helicopter was totaled, everyone was able to walk away.

Looking back, I saw a chain of events in this story leading to its conclusion. Of all the coyotes I've taken before or since, that small female was indeed the best coyote I've ever shot. It's funny how fate and life can intertwine in unexpected ways.

Do you know that feeling in your gut you sometimes get or that little voice in your ear? I learned to pay attention to those signs. Sometimes, you run late, or things go differently than planned. Those moments used to frustrate me until I realized that maybe, just maybe, everything really does happen for a reason.

Hughes 500 Helicopter

UH-OH !

NOW
WHAT DO WE DO?

CHAPTER 15

Uh-oh!
What Do We Do Now?

"When a snap of a twig causes the hair on the back of your neck to stand at attention..."

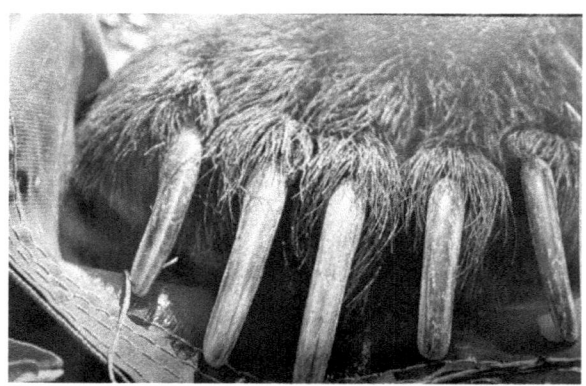

The goal was to collar and study the future reproduction of three sow grizzlies. In 2005, the U.S. Fish & Wildlife Service (USFWS), Tribal Fish and Game, and the Montana Fish Wildlife and Parks (MFWP) came together to work on this project along the Rocky Mountain Front. The study would help determine if bear numbers warranted delisting them from the threatened species list.

To help accomplish this project, Stan, the tribal bear manager, and his crew placed trail cameras near livestock carcasses in the foothills north of Browning. The motion-activated sensors would take pictures when a bear or other animal approached. When Stan obtained an image of a sow grizzly feeding at the site, he returned that afternoon and set up a tree stand. Just before dark, he climbed into the stand and attempted to dart and tranquilize the sow should she return. If successful, a GPS collar would be fitted onto the bear to monitor her activity and study birthrates over the next few years. This method worked well for him and was more selective than snaring.

One morning, while examining photos from the previous night, Stan noticed that besides bears, he had also captured pictures of four wolves feeding on a cow carcass. Stan called me after making the discovery, and we visited about what actions needed to be taken. We were worried as this area had an abundance of cattle, and game was scarce. After some discussion, we agreed to attempt to collar one of the wolves to monitor their movements. Setting traps with cattle in the pasture would be challenging, and the high concentration of grizzlies also concerned us.

After much thought, we devised a plan. I was confident in my ability to shoot a tranquilizer dart up to forty yards. Also, my supervisor, Greg, had an electronic call with a series of wolf howls. With this combination, calling a wolf close enough to dart and collar might work.

We arrived at the location in the foothills adjacent to Glacier National Park, a beautiful place where I never tired of working. Our first calling stand was a clearing in the thick pine trees a mile north of the bait where the wolf photos were taken. Greg, my supervisor, joined us that day. Stan, his tribal assistant Ron, and I completed the crew. The weather was perfect, a calm day with ideal conditions.

After walking a short distance from the pickup, we sat in the bushes on the edge of the clearing. Greg carried a shotgun for bear protection; Stan and I both had dart guns and pepper spray. I also brought along my .44 Magnum pistol, just in case.

Greg started the call, releasing a series of mournful howls. He continued calling periodically for another forty-five minutes with no sign of wolves. When finished, I suggested to Stan that we next try the clearing a mile south of the bait. He asked,

"What's wrong with the clearing below the bait where the wolf pictures were taken?"

I chuckled. "Have you forgotten about all those grizzly pictures taken along with the wolf ones?"

"I doubt a bear would come to a wolf howl," he told me. At that, I didn't know how to answer as I had never known anyone who had attempted this before.

We arrived at the calling location below the bait, wearing camouflage to help us hide in the foliage. I sat next to Greg while Stan positioned himself thirty yards to our right, and Ron sat in the bushes five yards behind us. The area was an open grassy clearing surrounded by thick trees.

Greg once again initiated the call with a long, drawn-out howl, and immediately, we heard the sound of something approaching from behind us. It didn't sound like a wolf; instead, it was something much larger, thirty to forty yards away in the thick pines. We heard twigs snap as a bear lumbered through the trees.

The actual location of where the bear approached us

In a hushed voice, Greg whispered, "That's a bear!"

This was scary, but we did have one thing in our favor: Greg had won the shotgun shooting contest at our state conference a week earlier. I knew he was a good shot but preferred not to witness firsthand if he could shoot bears as well as he shot clay pigeons.

The bear paused for a moment, then started coming our way again. We were unable to see it through the thick trees. If the bear walked out of the brush, it would be close enough that there would be little chance to escape a charge. Greg leaned closer and whispered, "What do you think?"

I responded, "I think I need a raise." I then stood up, followed by Greg and Ron. Stan, being somewhat hard of hearing, was looking south, still scanning for wolves, unaware of what was happening. I then turned to Ron and whispered, "Can you see the bear?"

"Nope," he said, "but he's pretty close."

"Do you have your pepper spray?" I asked.

He held up the pistol in his hand. "All I got today, Mike, is my lead spray."

Thankfully, detecting our presence, the bear stopped, remained invisible in the trees, and stalked away. With a sigh of relief, I walked over and tapped Stan on the shoulder, then told him what had happened. Afterward, we drove the pickup to the bait site, where we discovered photos of a large male grizzly feasting on the dead cow. He evidently had eaten and was resting when that pesky wolf started howling. We were all relieved to have it end this way. The time stamp showed the last picture of the bear was taken fifteen minutes before we started calling.

There was always room to learn. When I eventually retired, I still didn't know everything. The job was never dull; each day held a new and exciting experience.

Early in my career, I realized that regardless of what I said to Greg that day, I never was in this for the money.

CHAPTER 16

The Spooky Night Hunt at Heart Butte

"Darkness fell and its silence was broken only by the pounding of your heart and the unseen weight of fear lurking in the shadows."

My phone rang.

"Can you come up here with your night-vision rifle?" asked Stan, the bear specialist for the tribe, late one afternoon. Although my main job on the reservation was dealing with coyotes and, more recently, wolves, we often worked together to respond to bear problems.

The call was regarding a grizzly that had killed a cow and four calves within a week. Stan had set foot snares on the previous kills, but the bear was clever enough to dig them up. Clearly, this bear was no stranger to snares; it was a troublemaker.

Two nights prior, Stan had placed a trail camera on the latest victim, a cow. The following day, the snare was sprung, and he had only one picture of the culprit, a large male grizzly. Most cameras back then were equipped with a bright flash; since no other photos were taken, the flash must have spooked it. From there, the bear walked north a short distance and took down another calf.

It was summer and got dark around 10 p.m. that time of year. An hour later, I met Stan, and we drove a couple of miles from the small town of Heart Butte to a ranch house that belonged to the people who owned the cattle. There lived an elderly Blackfoot woman and her son.

We informed them what we were planning to do. After quietly listening, the old woman slowly approached me and rested her hand on my shoulder. "I will say a prayer for you," she whispered.

I could feel the power behind her words, and a peaceful feeling overcame me. I immediately felt better about what we needed to do. We hurriedly left for the kill site, as only an hour of daylight remained.

The calf lay in an open grassy bowl north of a grove of pines and was more than half consumed. It was an excellent location as it was seventy-five yards north of a low ridge of jack pines that ran east and west. The only drawback was that the pine trees were clustered, thin, and frail, too weak to climb. We would have to sit at their base on the ground when we returned to hunt the bear, a far more dangerous venture than perching safely in a tree. I jokingly told Stan he would owe me big time for this one.

Next, we drove south to the creek where the cow had been killed. After removing Stan's snares, we secured a chain to the cow's hind legs and pulled her with the pickup around the west side of the pine ridge. A soft wind was coming from the west. We thought if the bear went to the kill site first, it would follow the drag trail west of us, upwind from our location, and not catch our scent. We pulled the cow to rest alongside the dead calf and then drove to Heart Butte.

It was getting dark when we headed toward the home of the Blackfoot game warden, who lived two miles from town. I wanted to shoot my rifle (a 7mm Magnum with a night-vision scope) to make sure it was sighted in; there was little room for error that night.

After meeting the warden, we set up a cardboard box target at one hundred yards. I flipped the switch to activate the scope, but nothing happened! It came on after the second try. The switch didn't seem right, but I was glad it worked.

The Blackfoot warden was impressed when he looked through the scope. The optics were clear to one hundred yards but blurry beyond that. The terrain was lit up like early morning or late evening; the difference was everything had a ghostly green tint. A faint red cross marked the center. I sat down, positioned myself, and squeezed off a shot. The scope suddenly went black. I flipped the switch on and off and checked the battery, but it refused to turn back on.

We drove to Browning, hoping new batteries might solve the problem. New batteries were installed at the office, but we were disappointed to find it still wouldn't work. Later, after returning the scope to the factory, they discovered a bad wire connection. Fortunately, the scope problem had happened then instead of in the middle of our bear hunt. Looking back, there may have been a reason for that.

Stan had a portable spotlight, older night-vision goggles (similar to my scope but not as bright or clear), and a 300 Magnum rifle. I suggested we return to the kill site with his equipment and watch through the goggles. Should the bear return, I'd hold the light, and he could shoot it.

We made our way up the creek bottom in the dark. It was best to park and continue on foot for the last half mile so the grizzly would not see our pickup. A few hours had passed, and we worried the bear might have already been there and left. The night was pitch black, and I could barely see.

While walking in, I occasionally glanced through the night-vision goggles. Once we entered the trees, it was impossible to see any distance, and we prayed we didn't bump into a tree—or a bear. The wind muffled our approach; if the bear was nearby, it wouldn't hear us until we were next to it. My feelings were between excited and scared to death.

At the north edge of the trees, we sat on soft pine needles and peered through the night vision. Seventy-five yards away, the cow and calf remained undisturbed. I had my Benelli 12-gauge shotgun with slugs, and Stan, sitting on my left, had his rifle. The west wind was cold, and I was glad I brought my coveralls. Now, all we had to do was wait.

I constantly scanned with the goggles for the bear. After an hour and a half of sitting in the cold, I lifted the goggles and looked from right to left. Suddenly, standing to our left, less than twenty yards away was the silhouette of one of the biggest grizzlies I had ever seen! He was broadside and looking toward the dead cow, unaware of our presence. I lightly elbowed Stan and slowly handed him the goggles, whispering, "He's right there!"

I could hear my heartbeat and was sure I was listening to Stan's as well. Here we were, only twenty yards from the bear. Even though I had my shotgun, it was pitch black, and if the grizzly attacked, we would be defenseless. The bear had better night vision than we did, and I prayed he would remain focused on the cow and not spot us sitting under the trees.

After what felt like an eternity, Stan whispered, "He's on the carcass," and handed me the night-vision goggles. Looking through them, I could see the bear's silhouette, surrounded by green on the far side of the cow, facing toward us. I could hear the cow's flesh being torn away despite the wind blowing. I grabbed the spotlight and aimed it in the air. Whispering to Stan, I asked, "Are you ready?" When he said, "Yes," I clicked on the light and slowly lowered it toward the bear.

Seeing the light, the massive grizzly stood on its hind legs and stared directly at us. The illumination of the spotlight made the bear appear larger and much closer than it had in the night-vision goggles. Since all I could do was hold the light, I relied entirely on Stan to do his job. The bear then dropped on all fours—and Stan shot! I heard the thud of the bullet hitting its target.

The bear roared and began running to the east. Following him with the light, I thought, *If he goes over that ridge, we'll lose track of him.* It was total darkness except within the circle of light. While running, the grizzly looked over its right shoulder and, as if knowing the spotlight was the source of its trouble, suddenly turned and charged us.

We depended on each other. I trusted Stan to make the killing shot, and he relied on me to hold the light and not panic and run away; there was no room for error. We had been in tense situations before, but never anything like this. I thought, *Come on, Stan, don't miss.*

At fifty yards, he shot again, and the bullet hit the ground in front of the charging bear. Rocks flew up from the bullet's impact, hitting the bear. It was enough to cause him to turn and run west rather than toward us. Stan took aim, then shot again, and the bear rolled.

At that exact moment, the spotlight battery died!

It didn't fade away—it just went out!

Sitting in the dark, we were thankful it hadn't happened seconds before. Not wanting to approach the bear at that moment, there was nothing left to do but walk to the pickup and hope the last shot had finished the job. Despite it being far past midnight, our adrenaline was flowing and we were wide awake. Walking back, I nervously shone my dim flashlight around and wondered how many more bears might be lurking nearby.

When we returned, the bear lay motionless in the pickup's headlights. It was an eleven-year-old, five-hundred-pound male grizzly that had been in trouble and previously captured. Later that morning, the tribal wardens skinned the bear, gifting the hide to a Blackfeet elder.

Many years later, while visiting the elder's home, I was admiring a massive bear hide on his wall when the elder said, "I think you had something to do with this."

Mike—glad it's over!

With all the dangers we faced, I truly believed the old Blackfoot woman's prayers helped us that night. Her touch on my shoulder gave me a feeling that, to this day, remains unexplainable. Although it had been an unforgettable night, I was in no hurry to experience that again. From then on, whenever I saw Stan's name pop up on my caller ID, I couldn't help but hesitate before answering—never knowing what would happen next.

THE ELUSIVE GHOST
OF DUPUYER CREEK

CHAPTER 17

The Elusive Ghost of Dupuyer Creek

"The ghost of Dupuyer Creek moved in silence, its presence unnoticed for many days."

In May 2006, the Hayne Ranch near Dupuyer, Montana, was in the middle of lambing, the busiest time of the year for a sheep producer. It was the season that made the difference between success or failure, profit or loss, depending on factors like the weather, predators, the health of the sheep, and the level of effort put into the task.

After loading my four-wheeler one morning and looking forward to spending the day in the Sweet Grass Hills, I got a call from John, the owner of the Hayne Ranch. He told me he had found a ewe possibly killed by a grizzly.

So much for my trip north.

How fast my plans always seemed to change.

I pulled the four-wheeler out and loaded my bear equipment to meet John at his lambing pasture on Dupuyer Creek an hour later. Shortly afterward, Dave, from FWP, joined us.

We found the ewe lying in the middle of the large pasture. It had been torn open on the back end with minimal feeding, appearing as if it had died while being fed on by either coyotes or dogs during lambing.

At times, sheep had problems delivering and couldn't get up. With the lamb partially out, it had been eaten along with part of her back end. A large pool of blood covered the ground, indicating that this had happened while the sheep was still alive. I began skinning the ewe to verify my thoughts.

It was late morning; we were in the middle of an open meadow surrounded by tall willows and cottonwood trees working alongside our pickups. During my examination, John exclaimed, "Look, there's a coyote!"

I stood and spotted a pale-colored coyote walking through the sheep herd two hundred yards away. It passed ewes and lambs on its way to target a small bunch of lambs running and playing together. I quickly got my rifle from the pickup and found a steady rest. I didn't want to miss this shot, especially in front of these guys!

The coyote kept walking; we seemed invisible, and it never once looked in our direction. Before I could shoot, the coyote disappeared behind a low ridge. We knew exactly where it was by watching the head movement of the so-called guard llama. The llama should have been running the coyote out of the pasture. Instead, seemingly uninterested, the llama remained lying on a ridge thirty yards from the predator, showing no inclination to get up, let alone chase it.

By watching the llama, I could tell the coyote was returning to where it had come from. The llama's head followed its movement until the coyote emerged from behind the ridge with a freshly killed lamb hanging from its mouth and kept walking. At two hundred yards, it stopped; my rifle was ready.

In my dreams, I hunted more coyotes at night than during the day. At that moment, a recurring nightmare I had for years became a reality. I centered the coyote in my scope and squeezed the trigger—but the rifle didn't fire. I heard Dave softly remark, "There you go, shoot."

The coyote started walking, and I flipped the safety switch back and then forward to fire. I knew the gun had been off-safe, but tried this, hoping it would fix itself. The coyote paused again, and once more, I pulled the trigger, and again, the gun wouldn't fire. It felt like the trigger was locked.

The coyote approached the stand of willows and stopped one final time. The small dead lamb still hung from its mouth. I raised and lowered the rifle's bolt, thinking that might do something. I started lowering the crosshairs into place when suddenly, *BANG*! The gun went off on its own, firing just above the coyote before I was ready to shoot! (This was before I knew Remington was having problems with triggers on this particular rifle model.) Of all the times for this to happen, and worse yet, in front of an audience!

After I shot, the coyote dropped the lamb and ran into the willows. I was mad and embarrassed but not as angry as John. He used an electric fence for night penning, yet this coyote was killing in the middle of the day. We both knew this would continue until it was stopped, and I had just blown my chance. I was sure at that moment they were thinking it didn't take much to get my job. I tried explaining it was the rifle's fault but wasn't sure they believed me.

Grabbing a different rifle from my pickup, I walked toward the willows to search for the coyote. In the tall grass, I discovered a couple of lamb legs from previous kills and the limp dead lamb the coyote had just dropped. I didn't know how long this coyote had been killing or how many more lambs were about to be killed. One thing I did know: it was up to me to stop it.

After returning to the pickup, I told John I'd get the coyote one way or another. At that very moment, my cell phone rang, and what perfect timing! It was Tim, the helicopter pilot. He wanted to come over that evening and hunt the next day. (We took turns flying in those days, and it so happened to be my turn.)

I met the helicopter at my house later that afternoon. This was my only option, as the sheep scattered throughout the pasture made it impossible to set equipment. And with all the grizzlies lurking around, attempting to call it in would be dangerous.

That evening at dusk, we flew the creek coming from the east. I had never looked so hard for a coyote in my life. Tim was the perfect person to fly with. He was not only a great pilot but had sharp vision as well. We flew over the willow tops, back and forth, side to side, like a bird dog. We hunted for an hour and shot a couple of coyotes in the vicinity, but none were white. The trees and willows were leafed out, which made visibility a challenge. Flying home that evening, I hoped we would be successful the next day, as Tim would have to leave after our flight.

Early the following day, we flew west up the creek bottom. If the coyote was hidden in the willows, like the evening before, it would be a problem. In places, the willows grew twelve to fourteen feet tall and were so dense I wouldn't be able to see a bear running through them, let alone a coyote.

We flew into the pasture at twice the height of a telephone pole. On the south side of the sheep in the willows two hundred yards from John's house, I caught a flash of white.

It was the coyote.

Tim hurried the helicopter; ahead of us, the coyote, running as fast as it could, exited the willows and emerged into a small opening.

I held the shotgun out the window with Tim flying the helicopter at top speed. Very seldom have I been more determined to get a coyote. My shotgun was a 12-gauge semi-automatic with copper-plated BBs capable of firing as quickly as I could pull the trigger. I had one shell in the chamber and seven in the magazine. The coyote was a long way ahead of us and running fast when I fired the first shot.

I typically didn't shoot at coyotes from that distance, but this was our only opportunity, and it would soon disappear in the thick willows. To both our surprise, the coyote rolled. As we got closer, I quickly fired four more shots to make sure the animal was dead. I couldn't believe we had been so fortunate to find it in this jungle. Later that day, after we landed, I called John with the good news; I'm not sure which of us was more relieved.

The following day, after meeting John, we walked into the willows to get a look at this lamb-killing coyote. As we entered the clearing, it reminded me of a movie I had seen about African lions, where the hunters discovered their lair littered with human bones. In this case, the lair was full of the remains of dozens of lambs.

We found the small, light-colored, dry female coyote in the middle of it all. Despite the abundance of natural prey, this coyote preferred eating lambs. It was impossible to determine how many she had previously killed or would have continued to kill had we not stopped her.

Usually, coyotes hunted at night, early morning, or evening. This one had John's pattern figured out; she would exit the willows as soon as he left the sheep in the middle of the day. She'd then kill and carry a lamb into the willow patch to feed.

She was like a ghost, and her secret might have never been discovered had she not shown herself that day.

THERE
One Minute
GONE
The Next

CHAPTER 18

There One Minute, Gone the Next

"A brief encounter, a critical mistake, and so close to a disaster..."

In early June 2008, Don, a sheep producer, called to tell me that bears had killed several of his sheep south of Choteau, Montana. This wasn't the first time he had experienced bear problems at that location, so I wasn't surprised.

The sheep were grazing on forty acres of river bottom fifty miles away. I arrived and met Don, Dave, and the local FWP game warden at the site. Don told us that he had discovered thirteen ewes killed and two others alive with the udders eaten the previous morning. Those two had been put down, bringing the number to fifteen. Six lambs had also been killed, and Don figured that many more were either missing or would likely die due to losing their mothers in the bear attack. Some, he thought, might have drowned in the river.

He explained that after making the discovery, he had dragged some of the dead sheep below a tree stand in the middle of the pasture used for hunting whitetail deer. The stand sat in a tree twenty feet high. At the time, he had thought stray dogs might have been responsible and planned to shoot them should they return. He waited in the tree stand all night and saw nothing. At daylight, he examined the carcasses again and changed his mind, thinking a grizzly bear might be the culprit. That's when Don had decided to call me.

Investigating the kills, I found his story somewhat strange, as it was obvious this was the work of a bear. Nearby, we found tracks of two young grizzlies measuring five and a half inches across, confirming my suspicions.

Don had lost several other ewes to a grizzly bear at this location two years before. I had captured the problem bear the first night at the kill site. Since it was a male and had caused problems before, it was euthanized. Even though the bears weren't as plentiful back then, I explained that this was a perfect location for an attack to happen again and that he should reconsider where to graze his sheep or find a way to protect them.

Tall, ancient cottonwood trees surrounded by willows and thick brush lined the river bottom. In foliage like that, bears usually traveled a short distance to bed down after making a kill, and I felt I had an excellent chance of capturing one or both by morning. Don and the warden helped me load the dead sheep into a pickup, holding back two for bait. It was not an easy task. They then assisted me in setting four foot snares. With the bears nearby, I was happy to have the help and even happier to have someone to watch my back.

After the snares were set, Don mentioned, "Look, so I received this letter from a wildlife organization that compensates for livestock killed by grizzlies. They paid for my earlier kills."

"Yeah?" I asked, not surprised.

"But they're not going to pay for future losses," Don continued with a frown. "Not unless I took measures to protect the sheep." He sighed, deeply unhappy. "You think they'll cover this mess?"

Knowing he *hadn't* taken those precautions and not wanting to commit to an answer, I shrugged. "That's a really good question."

The pasture was too large and brushy for electric fencing, but a small electric night pen to bed the sheep would be possible. Unfortunately, he lived fifty miles away, making running back and forth twice a day to lock the sheep up at night and let them out in the morning difficult. Guard dogs weren't an option either, as it was too close to town with neighbors nearby; they would only get into trouble. After weighing our options, we decided to construct a temporary electric bed ground to protect the sheep for a few nights to help in my efforts to capture the bears.

Despite living fifty miles away, I arrived at the trap site as dawn approached. The snares were in thick brush and trees, and I had to walk through a jungle to check them.

When checking bear snares, if the wind wasn't blowing, I always sat in the pickup for a few minutes before walking in. If a bear was captured, I could usually hear it vocalizing its frustration, giving me a heads-up.

After listening for a while and hearing nothing, I took my shotgun and pepper spray and carefully walked in to check. My snares were empty. The bears had not returned, and I couldn't figure out why. The snares remained set for two more nights with no results.

There had to be more to this story, more going on here.

On the third day, after checking empty snares, I met Dave at the trap site. That morning, I had brought my metal detector on a hunch. Turning it on, I searched the tall grass at the base of the tree stand. My detector sounded, and I found an empty .300 Weatherby Magnum cartridge. It was older and looked like it had been fired the year before. Then, mere inches away, the detector beeped again. This time, I found an empty shotgun shell. It was fresh, and on the side was marked "3-inch Magnum Slugger," an ideal cartridge for hunting bears.

Finally, an explanation as to why the bears had not returned.

What a waste of time and money! I didn't enjoy waking up every morning at 3:30 a.m., driving over fifty miles, dodging deer in the dark, to trap ghosts.

The first thing I did was call my supervisor. I told him what I had discovered and decided to pull the snares. He agreed. Next, I called Don, telling him about the shotgun shell and that the snares would be removed. He then told me what had happened.

At 9 p.m. on the evening the kills were discovered, he had settled in the tree stand above the dead sheep to wait for the dogs. As it was getting dark, he spotted a beaver swimming in the river fifty yards away. Deciding to check the accuracy of his shotgun, he shot at it, which is why the shotgun casing was there.

I found the story difficult to believe. To start with, the river was running high and almost black in color. There was no way beavers would swim in that fast-moving water under those conditions. I then asked, "Why would you spend all afternoon dragging dead sheep under that tree stand to lure in whatever had killed them, only to ruin your chance by shooting at a beaver around the time the culprit might return? Plus, if you were going to shoot a dog up close, buckshot would have worked much better than slugs."

He explained that he had carried both kinds of shells that night.

Everything about the story was fishy.

I decided to leave the snares set one final night. Don met me early the following day, unhappy that I was leaving. I had already removed the snares and told him that if the bear returned, I would set them again.

"In the meantime," I said, slinging a snare into the back of my truck, "if they were my sheep, I'd get them out of here or find some way to protect them."

Neither was accomplished, and to no one's surprise, three weeks later, more sheep were killed.

Don usually checked his sheep only once a week. Early July, he called, explaining that he'd found the remains of four ewes and three lambs. Upon my investigation, it was evident that the kills had occurred over the previous few days.

Near the dead sheep, I discovered the same smaller five-and-a-half-inch tracks, but this time, it looked as if only one bear had been present. The kills had been made in thick vegetation, one hundred fifty yards from the closest place I could access with my pickup. Using two dead sheep for bait, I set foot snares with the warden's assistance, and we removed the remaining sheep. It was a lot of work, trudging through the thick brush and fighting mosquitos every step of the way.

The following two mornings, my snares remained empty. When I parked the pickup on the third day and rolled down the window, I could hear the unmistakable bawl of a bear captured in a snare. What a relief it was to be greeted by that sound and to know the ordeal would soon end.

I called Dave to share the news. We had previously decided that if it was a male, it would get no other chances. If it was a sow, it would get one more. The bear would first have to be tranquilized to determine its fate.

Shotguns in hand, we walked toward the captured bear. It was necessary to get close enough to estimate its weight to determine the quantity of drug required. My heart raced as we made our way through the thick brush. Dense vegetation and trees limited our visibility. Making matters worse, the morning sun shone through the branches directly in our eyes as we walked down the narrow trail, approaching the bear from the west. I knew the way in from this direction; it was our only route.

Looking toward the snare site, taken from alongside Mike's pickup

As we drew closer to the snare site, I kept thinking there was a good chance this wasn't the only bear. We had found evidence of only one bear on this second go-around, but there had initially been two. I had the shotgun ready, half expecting the snared bear's partner to charge out of the brush at any moment. Another concern was that we were unsure how well this bear had been caught in the snare; we'd have to be close to find out. Slowly and cautiously, we approached.

We found out later that the neighbors living nearby had heard the bear get caught the night before at 11 p.m. That meant it had been snared for roughly eight hours. Usually, bears became tuckered out after that much time, but as this one came into view, we found that not to be the case. It was worked up as any bear I'd ever seen, jumping up and down, back and forth.

Then, I saw something out of the ordinary. Bears often swiped at snares, trying to get it off. However, this bear was lying on his back, methodically attempting to remove the snare from its wrist with the claws of his free paw. That greatly concerned me, and I mentioned this to Dave, who assured me there was nothing to worry about... but worry I did.

We estimated the bear's weight and returned to the pickup to prepare the dart. Halfway there, all went quiet. While loading the dart, it fell eerily silent. As we made our way back to the trap site, I mentioned to Dave how strange it was that we hadn't heard one sound over the last half hour. Dave told me he thought the bear was exhausted after being caught for most of the night and was likely resting.

As we stepped into the small clearing, I looked toward the torn-up ground where the bear had once been, and as I had feared, it was gone. The empty snare lay on the ground.

The torn-up capture site

Looking back, it was fortunate we hadn't been present when the bear escaped. The story could have ended much differently.

By now, everyone knew what we were doing, and I was sure word of the bear's escape would spread and hit all the papers. I examined the snare to determine what went wrong. The snare consisted of a quarter-inch cable equipped with an L-lock. The L-lock had two holes drilled into it. One hole was larger where the cable's end was attached to the lock. The other was a smaller-diameter hole where the snare cable slid to tighten around the bear's leg. I had constructed most of these snares, but others had been supplied by the agency; I was not sure who had made this one.

Further examination of the snare revealed the problem. The lock was reversed with the bigger hole on the sliding side, meaning it would not stay tight after cinching around the bear's wrist. The grizzly must have hooked a long claw in the loop and loosened the snare to release itself. Later that day, I examined snares that had previously caught bears at my house. I found one with the same mistake. Fortunately, that bear hadn't escaped; it was a lesson learned.

The story of the bear spread like wildfire. I had to hand it to Dave, who never revealed the lock issue or how the bear escaped. People love a story when something goes wrong; this was no exception. Soon, it reached the newspapers, TV, and radio stations, stating, "Veteran Trapper Loses Grizzly."

For months afterward, when my name was Googled, that was the first story to appear. All the success stories were hidden below. The rancher was never compensated for the thousands of dollars he lost, and sheep never grazed in that pasture again.

Many have advocated making it legal for livestock owners to shoot bears that cause problems. Under certain circumstances, they should have that right. In the same respect, however, they should first utilize all possible methods to protect their animals, especially sheep. But in this case, guard dogs were not the solution, and building fencing would have been nearly impossible.

For days afterward, the coffee shop crowd couldn't stop talking about what had happened. I guess if they were talking about me, they weren't talking about someone else.

This episode was just another segment of my continuing education. Because of a simple snare lock, things could have gone terribly wrong, but thankfully, they didn't.

CHAPTER 19

Fishing for Bears

*"The only lure here is your adrenaline,
riding every snap of a twig."*

June 5, 2009, marked my thirty-first anniversary working for Wildlife Services. Just when I thought I'd seen it all on the job, that evening I had an experience that will remain with me for the rest of my life.

Early that morning, I drove to the Reservation and met Stan, the tribal bear biologist. Our destination was a beautiful spot north of Browning that had the highest number of wolves in my district and always will. In the past, we had spent countless hours there responding to wolf/cattle depredations.

A one-month-old calf had been bitten and injured by what looked to be a single wolf. Our only job was to document and verify the injury. There was no financial compensation for injured livestock. However, if documented, the rancher would be compensated for the loss if it later died. No equipment was set since there wasn't a kill to trap on. Afterward, it was time for Stan to remove his wolf hat and put on his bear hat.

The Northern Continental Divide Ecosystem Grizzly Bear Population Monitoring Program was to take place on the East Front of the Rockies that summer. Dave, the state MFWP bear specialist, was required to capture three sows to the south and equip them with GPS radio collars. Stan, the tribal biologist on the Reservation, was responsible for collaring an equal number of bears to the north. MFWP set foot snares to capture bears

The back foot of a grizzly

until the required three sows were collared. Boars and cubs were simply released if accidentally caught.

I wasn't a fan of this method because it made it more difficult for me to respond to livestock depredations if the offending bear was snare-wise. Because of this, Stan took a different approach toward the collaring project and tried to avoid educating bears about snares. His job was not only to capture them for research but on depredations as well. I had heard about his collaring method for years and had always wanted to see firsthand how it was accomplished.

After verifying the injured calf north of Browning, Stan asked if I would like to accompany him that evening to dart and collar a sow coming into one of the bait sites, and I readily accepted.

In three locations, the tribal bear crew had previously put out baits (dead horses, cows, etc.). Trail cameras were also placed and checked daily. From the pictures, they could verify how many bears were present and at what time they had arrived at the bait. They would then study the bears in the photos to determine if a sow grizzly was present.

After it was established that a desired bear was coming to the baits, that evening, a tree stand was placed sixteen feet above the smorgasbord of dead livestock. The goal was to sit above the baits with a dart gun and tranquilize and collar the target bear when it returned.

This procedure was accomplished with two or three people, one in the stand and one or two others in a pickup. After dropping off the darter (usually Stan), his assistants helped him access the tree stand with a ladder. They then drove a mile away to wait for Stan to radio news of the bear being darted or to say the hunt was over. This method was often successful; he had collared many bears this way without a problem.

Stan's dart gun was equipped with a medium-sized open-bale fishing reel attached to the bottom of the barrel. A heavy yellow line ran down the end of the barrel and attached to the back of the tranquilizer dart. A laser sight was connected to the side of the barrel and equipped with a button to turn it on when he was ready to fire. When the targeted sow arrived, the laser was turned on, and the red dot was placed on the bear where he wanted the dart to penetrate. Once darted, some bears stayed in place, wondering what had happened, while other bears spooked and ran a short distance with the yellow line trailing behind them.

Once the dart connected, Stan radioed the others and they waited for fifteen minutes. Next, they cautiously followed the line to the drugged bear. It was always best if this happened before nightfall. After dark, they could follow the yellow line with a flashlight or headlamp.

What made nighttime suspenseful, however, was that they never knew if other bears were lurking about. There was also the possibility that the darted bear was not completely tranquilized and waiting for them at the end of the line in the darkness.

I was excited as we drove to our destination that afternoon. To the west, the Rocky Mountains towered over us, and the border to Glacier National Park was not far away. The Reservation had always been my favorite place; I loved working there and enjoyed being with its people.

It was a rough trail through dense trees to reach the bait site. The carcasses I saw when we arrived were putrid and crawling with maggots. Even though I was used to being around that kind of thing, it was still overwhelming. We then set up two tree stands, prepared the dart gun, and slipped on camouflage clothing. It was a perfect evening to dart a bear.

At 6:30 p.m., Rick, Stan's co-worker, helped us access our tree stands with a ladder. I had my pistol, but just before I climbed up, Rick handed me a can of pepper spray. He explained that if a bear spotted me and tried coming up the tree, I could spray it in the face to deter it. I realized that was a great idea.

The pictures from that morning revealed that four grizzlies and several black bears had been present the previous night. The first grizzly on the camera had arrived at 9 p.m. while it was still daylight. From the photos, it looked to be a breeding-age female. If she returned, we stood a good chance of collaring our bear before dark.

It was 7 p.m. when we settled in the stands, and our assistant drove away. Should the sow come in after dark, Stan had with him night-vision goggles that would work well with the laser sight.

We were situated above the dead and decaying cows, which gave off a powerful odor.

Fortunately, a light breeze was blowing to the west, away from our tree stands.

Unfortunately, that breeze was not enough to keep away the hordes of hungry mosquitoes that swarmed all around us.

We had sat in the tree stands for only ten minutes when, out of nowhere, a black bear appeared below us. Suddenly, I didn't notice the pesky mosquitos anymore. Watching the animal, I thought about how much people would pay for this experience. The bear strolled to the bait pile ten yards away and started eating, oblivious to our presence. Despite working with bears for almost two decades, I had never witnessed anything like this before; it was fascinating to watch.

After a few minutes, the bear stepped back, froze, and intently stared to the west. We listened and watched as the black bear left as swiftly as it had appeared. A couple of minutes later, in the vegetation before us, we could hear the sound of another approaching bear.

Thick brush and trees surrounded the small clearing in every direction, limiting our visibility. The undergrowth moved and shook as the bear drew closer. Then, I heard the unmistakable sound of popping jaws and clicking teeth, signs of an agitated grizzly; this had to be the sow.

As the bear came into view, I spotted her brown silhouette in the bushes, thirty yards away. It was the medium-sized sow we were after. However, instead of heading straight toward the baits, the bear moved parallel, lumbering east. She was in the underbrush, and at that distance, while moving, it would have been difficult to hit her with a tranquilizer dart. She must have caught wind of us because she kept walking, sensing something was wrong. The bear disappeared in the thick foliage, and all we could do was sit there, hoping she would return.

After a few minutes, two medium-sized black bears appeared. Even though I was sore from sitting on the metal tree stand and unhappy being constantly attacked by mosquitos, I never grew bored watching the fascinating scene before me.

After those two finished eating, a tiny black bear came ambling in. I really enjoyed watching this little guy. However, it only fed a few minutes before it hurriedly ran off. Soon, I saw why: ambling up the trail like a sumo wrestler was one of the largest black bears I had ever seen! It weighed at least four hundred pounds and grunted like a pig when it walked.

This bear spent the most time eating. Watching how it fed and effortlessly dragged the heavy carcass around was mesmerizing. I could hear other bears moving through the thick brush around us while it ate, afraid to challenge this monster. Evidently, no grizzlies were around, or they would have cut his meal short.

The bear kept eating until after dark. I could no longer see the scene but could hear the bear tear flesh from the carcass as it ate. Beyond the bear, Stan, with his night-vision goggles, spotted two wolves. They were in the exact location the sow grizzly had passed earlier, thirty yards out. They either knew we were there or were leery of the bear before us as they stayed only a couple minutes and left.

We sat in the tree stand for another hour. The bears came and went, but they were all blacks. With the aid of night-vision, Stan watched everything. All I could see in the starlight was an occasional glimpse of a ghostly black silhouette silently passing below my tree stand. I never got bored, and my heart raced to hear the bears feed, twigs snap, and brush break as who knows how many other bears circled around us.

After sitting in the tree stand in the constant presence of bears for five hours, a lone black bear was still feeding below us at midnight. Stan whispered, "My eyes are tired and blurry, making it hard to see; I think we're done." He then shined his flashlight toward the bear feeding underneath our feet. The bear briefly looked our way unconcerned and acting like it was only looking at the moon. Stan then called Rick to come get us. While waiting, we quietly visited, and the bear kept feeding. It finally left when the lights of the approaching pickup shone up the road.

Rick grabbed a ladder from the back and helped us down from our stands. While loading our equipment, we heard bears circling, waiting for us to get out of the way so they could feed again. Their unseen presence and the sound of them walking through the brush in the dark gave me an eerie feeling.

That evening was one of the most exciting nights of my life. Later that summer, the Tribe went on to dart and collar the three required grizzly bears, but I never had the chance to repeat that unforgettable experience.

Time flew by so fast; Stan retired, and a few years later, so did I. Things change, and most of the people I worked with are now gone. However, a fond memory remains of a warm June night, sitting in a tree stand, fishing for bears.

CHAPTER 20

Dahlie, My Most Terrifying Experience

"The grizzly's presence was undeniable, its movement calculated and direct. This was the moment I had prepared for my entire life!"

In my job, receiving a call at 6 a.m. was never welcomed as usually something bad had happened.

I received such a call in May 2009 from a woman who lived along Sheep Creek on the Rocky Mountain Front. She spoke quickly, breathlessly; it didn't take long to understand why.

Early that morning, Elena had awakened to a strange noise from the barn a short distance from her house and so went to investigate. They owned four llamas, and she noticed two were standing to the south and one to the north of the barn; the fourth was missing.

As she drew closer, she spotted it between the brush-filled creek and the barn. But then it did something totally unexpected for a llama. It stood on its back legs and growled!

The llama was there all right, but a four-hundred-pound grizzly bear was feeding on it. Since the bear was the same shade of brown as the llama and she hadn't been wearing her glasses, it wasn't until the bear stood that she realized what was happening. Elena froze in fear as the bear locked eyes with her forty yards away. Slowly, she backed toward the safety of her house, praying the bear would not attack. That's when she called the government trapper.

The remains of the grizzly-killed llama

When I arrived, I found the dead llama had been halfway consumed. Blood covered the ground, and bite marks were located on the back and forehead. As llamas are curious creatures, it looked as if this one had walked up to the bear and simply been attacked.

After examining the scene, I moved the remains of the llama into the willows fifty yards away, where I placed a foot snare at the entrance to a pen set. I then put a pipe snare set at the kill site, placing llama meat inside for bait. Just as I finished, it started to snow—and continued snowing throughout the day and into the night until two and a half feet covered the ground.

Over the next few days, the bear did not return. However, I knew it was only a matter of time before it would. I removed my snares, and three weeks later, Elena called again to inform me that another llama had been killed. Again, I set a pipe snare at the kill site and dragged the remains to the creek bottom, where a foot snare was placed at the same pen set. The snow was gone, and I figured it was only a matter of time before the bear would be caught if we didn't run out of llamas first.

I rose early the following day, and while driving to check the sets at 5:30 am, my cell phone rang. It was Diane; we had caught the bear. The heads-up was appreciated so I could alert FWP and get them on their way.

The four-hundred-pound male had been caught in the pipe set. He was clearly not happy to have a cable around his wrist. I was thankful I had attached such a large amount of weight to the snare cable. The creek was nearby and running high after the recent snowfall. The weights would keep it anchored and prevent it from going in that direction.

We judged the bear's weight, and Dave mixed the tranquilizer. Often, we could drive slowly up to a bear and dart it from the pickup's passenger side. At other times, walking in was necessary. The pickup method was always best, but not without risk, especially with an angry bear like this one. He was the maddest bear I had ever seen.

The grizzly stared intently at us as I eased the pickup closer. From the passenger side, Dave put the dart gun out the window. He aimed carefully and fired, hitting the bear in the front shoulder.

The bear stood on its hind legs, quickly came down, and then charged the pickup. Thank God something didn't break or he didn't escape the snare. He toppled over ten yards away, stopped by the end of the snare cable. I guarantee that bear would have come through the window. I slammed the pickup in reverse, relieved that the drug had been administered.

That was the crankiest bear I had ever witnessed in a snare and not one I would want to meet on the creek bottom. After that day, I began holding a can of pepper spray while Dave darted in case one of these unpredictable bears escaped and tried to join us in the front seat.

Once the bear went down, the operation was routine. It was a four-year-old male. We took measurements and radio-collared, ear-tagged, and PIT-tagged him by inserting a small chip under his hide to be read with a scanner for identification purposes. Finally, we weighed the bear; this was accomplished using a heavy tarp with rings hooked to a scale and elevated with the FWP crane attached to the pickup. Since this was a first capture, the bear was placed into a culvert trap and relocated by FWP to the west side of the Continental Divide, approximately eighty miles away.

It took the bear only a short time to find its way home.

We located the signal two weeks later.

A few days after that, he slipped the FWP telemetry collar. It was frustrating after all the time and effort, not to mention risking our lives. That was the only way to keep track of him. We knew all along that this bear would be a problem. We were proven right just a short time later.

During July, while I was on vacation, Steve, the Great Falls specialist who was covering for me, responded to yet another llama depredation on Sheep Creek. The location was five miles east of where the bear had been captured. This guard llama, belonging to a different producer, was killed and mostly consumed several days before being discovered. Because of this, it was too late to set snares. However, they were confident this was a kill and was likely made by the same bear that had killed the previous two llamas.

A few days later, Steve received *another* complaint and found a bear had slipped under the electric fence and killed three ewes in the same pasture. He constructed a foot snare pen set this time, but the bear did not return. They thought the culprit got shocked exiting the electric fence and was hesitant to return.

Another llama was purchased, and the sheep and new llama remained in the electrified pasture until September with no further losses. The flock was then relocated to a wheat stubble field two miles away.

The bear took little time to discover the new location and found no electric fence there to protect them. Just two days after the sheep had settled in, three ewes were killed. After examining the kills, I felt certain my old friend had returned.

I went to work, removing two dead sheep and dragging the third to my set location. Next, a pen was erected using a snow fence to encircle the sheep, and a foot snare was placed in the opening. That night, the bear returned, but unfortunately, instead of going through the open space, it simply tore down the side of the pen and removed the sheep. The next day, after witnessing this, I put another layer of snow fence on top of the existing pen, making the sides eight feet high.

The bear returned the following night and once again pulled down the side of the pen to feast on mutton.

He was smarter than the average bear.

I went to work placing a blind set adjacent to the pen and another hidden snare on the path leading toward the site. At daylight the next morning, nothing was captured, and that afternoon, I discovered the reason why.

After the snares were checked that morning, the rancher had searched for but couldn't locate his new llama. That evening, he discovered it on the creek bottom. Yet, another victim. He gave me a call, and I hurried the thirty-five miles back to the site. This location was much better to set, but it was getting late. Thick trees and willows with many trails made it a perfect place to put in blind trail sets, which worked well for trap-wise bears. While circling the kill, the bear would unknowingly step into the snare loop discreetly set in the trail.

While setting the snares, I heard gunshots reverberate around me. I then remembered it was opening day of youth deer season. If all the gunshots and activity didn't run the bear out of the area, the gut piles would keep him well-fed with no need to return to the kill site. I knew, either way, my chances of success were dwindling.

The bear never returned, and the snares were removed.

Winter came, but I was sure this wasn't the end of it. When spring arrived, I knew Dahlie would return. A co-worker had given this bear the name Dahlie, like the famous Dalai Lama. Never before or since had we seen a bear with a taste for llamas like this one. While performing necropsies, I noticed that llama meat smelled similar to lamb. It made sense why he found them so tasty.

That spring, the two FWP bear specialists were snaring along the East Front, attempting to place GPS collars on three sows for the population-monitoring study. Checking snares one morning, Dave found two bears caught in one location at the base of the mountains. Both were large boars, and one of the bears was Dahlie. Dave explained later that he had debated euthanizing Dahlie on the spot because of his numerous strikes. Instead, he installed a new radio collar and released him.

Dave called to inform me of the situation; I wasn't pleased. He said that if Dahlie came down Dupuyer Creek and started killing sheep again, we would utilize telemetry to find and shoot him. I always hated sneaking through dense willows to hunt grizzly bears. I was disappointed and felt Dave should have handled the situation when the bear was caught in the research snare.

During the first part of June 2010, a month after the research capture, my phone rang at 6:30 a.m. This time, it was a rancher west of Conrad, forty miles from the mountainfront and seven air miles from my house. The rancher claimed wolves had entered the corral and killed several sheep. I thought it was probably dogs, as this wasn't prime wolf habitat, but I placed a couple of wolf traps in my pickup just in case.

One of the ewes killed in the corral

An hour later, I met his wife, and we walked to the corral. Looking at the carnage, I told her we would need bigger traps. Three ewes were on their backs, their briskets and udders eaten. One more was killed and not consumed. Three small lambs were dead but not fed on. Four other lambs would later die as they were too small to survive without their mother and too big to want a bottle.

This had been the work of a bear.

After looking for tracks, I searched the fence line for hair samples. I found a place in the fence where the grizzly had gone under and collected its hair for DNA analysis. After returning home to get bear equipment, I started setting snares.

Dave and his assistant, Jared, showed up a couple of hours later. I mentioned I was unable to find tracks but had collected hair samples. While I set snares, they searched for tracks along the creek. Even though it was miles away, I had a hunch Dahlie had been responsible. His front track had measured six and a half inches the previous year. But they reported back to me that the tracks they discovered were five-and-three-quarters inch. It looked like we were dealing with a different bear.

I had time to set three snares. Two were walk-through sets using large round straw bales with a pathway between them. A sheep carcass was placed in the middle to lure the bear down the path. I also put in a pipe set along with two trail cameras.

That night, around midnight, I was awakened by the sound of coyotes howling near my house. Most of our sheep were grazing at a ranch a mile west, but we had a flock of ram lambs at home. I opened the bedroom window to determine what direction the coyotes were howling from. As quickly as I started listening, they stopped howling. The night was quiet, allowing me to hear the faint sound of the neighbor's guard dogs barking furiously three miles to the west.

The rancher who owned the dogs ran approximately a thousand sheep and was only two miles west of my ewes. Listening to the dogs' frantic barking, I knew where the bear was and whose sheep it was killing.

I slept some, but by 4:30 a.m., I was ready to go. It was getting daylight as I passed the farm where my sheep grazed. They usually bedded around the outbuildings next to the farmer's house. However, the sheep were out in the pasture that morning, huddled together in a tight circle and acting nervous. I stopped, looking over the grassy field to the east, and wondered if coyotes had spooked them. Until now, there hadn't been a known grizzly bear in my area for over a century. Eventually, the sheep started grazing, so I lost my concern.

Just beyond the farmer's house, the road crossed the canal alongside a large shelter belt of trees. Driving by, looking to the south, I was shocked to see an enormous grizzly running through an open field five hundred yards away.

In hindsight, it's possible it had startled my sheep, bunching them up, and had been ready to kill before hearing my pickup. The bear ran into the trees while I was watching the sheep and, afterward, crossed the road.

When I spotted the grizzly, the light was dim, and I couldn't see if the bear wore a collar. It looked dark, but the actual color was hard to determine because of the light conditions. I watched until it disappeared and then left a voicemail for Dave. Seeing that bear, there was no doubt the snares were empty, but they still needed to be checked.

After checking snares, I went to the ranch, where the guard dogs had been barking the night before. I figured I'd find more sheep depredations and wasn't disappointed. Searching the pasture, I found one ewe killed, mostly eaten, with her two small lambs huddled by her side. Ironically, that sheep had been attacked while under the watch of guard dogs. Dogs usually worked when dealing with younger bears; however, older bears were often not intimidated by their presence. Who knew though? Maybe the bear would have killed more ewes had the dogs not been present that night.

The rancher was upset when I informed him of the discoveries. He told me he didn't want snares set and only wanted to see the bear dead. This was the first time in anyone's memory that a grizzly had been this far east killing sheep. Many of the ranches in the area had been established in the late 1800s and had not dealt with anything like this for years.

I went home and wondered what to do next. I told the rancher to consider setting snares and that I would call him in the afternoon. This was going to be a challenge. I was dealing with an intelligent bear that liked to kill sheep. Setting snares the day before had been unsuccessful as the bear did not return.

It would be futile to trap at the second ranch as the sheep were scattered over a vast area. All the bear needed to do was go into the pasture and make a fresh kill, never having to return to the previous one. Also, several other sheep ranches were in the area (including mine), providing plenty of other sheep to choose from.

Early that afternoon, the phone rang. It was Dave. He had been flying that morning along the Rocky Mountain Front, checking locations of radio-collared bears. He had received my phone message about the bear. Searching near the last kill site on the Dry Fork, using telemetry, he found our old friend Dahlie, who was bedded in a patch of willows next to the sheep pasture, resting for the next night's adventure.

Evidently, the tracks they had measured the day before were incorrect.

"Is your bear rifle ready?" Dave asked.

He had just phoned the U.S. Fish and Wildlife Service and been granted permission to remove the bear. Jared would also come along. We would meet at my house that afternoon. Dave planned to operate the telemetry receiver to locate the bear, and I would shoot it; that was the plan. Since the bear had a radio collar, we should have no problem finding him.

A decade earlier, I had bought a 300 Weatherby Magnum rifle specifically for bears. After the purchase, I took my new gun to sight it in. It was light in weight and kicked like a mule. Even with a recoil shield on my shoulder, I got a headache after a few shots. Once I finished sighting it in, I had stored the rifle in the gun cabinet and hoped never to torture myself in that way again.

After the call, I took the rifle north of the house to squeeze off a couple of shots before their arrival. I placed a box at one hundred yards and shot twice using an extended bipod that stabilized the gun. Both shots were an inch-and-a-half high off my one-inch target drawn in the center of the box. The bullet holes touched each other. It didn't get much better than that. I was glad it would only take two shots, as my shoulder was already sore.

I went home and eagerly awaited their arrival. Dave and Jared got to the house at 5 p.m. Dave shared pictures taken from the plane that morning of the bear bedded in a willow patch. I knew the exact location; it was on a creek bottom, just one hundred yards west of a seldom-used county road five miles from my house.

The creek bottom was a couple hundred yards wide. Scattered cottonwood trees and willows lined its banks. Once there, we activated the telemetry receiver three hundred yards north of where the bear had been discovered. The loud *beep-beep* of the telemetry told us it was still there.

Our plan was to drive beyond the sleeping bear a quarter of a mile. I would then sneak over and lie atop a low ridge on the south side of the creek, one hundred yards away. I wished I had my electronic call with bear sounds, but it was getting repaired. I believed if I played it, the bear would have stood up, and I could have shot him. But then we would have missed out on all the excitement yet to come.

I carried a handheld radio and was to click the mic twice when I was ready and in place. They were to head north, back across the creek, with the pickup. Jared was to walk in, and we hoped he'd run the bear out of its day bed in my direction. Jared would have his rifle, but it had been decided that I would get the first shot.

Lying on the ridge, I peered toward the willows and watched Jared's careful approach. Soon, he disappeared into the willow patch, and Dave began walking in from the east. A sense of anticipation ran through me as I realized that soon something exciting was about to happen.

Then suddenly, the bear jumped up, but instead of coming toward me as we had hoped, he dashed west up the creek. The bear had over two hundred yards of open terrain until the next willow patch. He had slowed to a lope and glanced back occasionally toward Jared; I thought he might even stop. At one hundred yards, I had an excellent chance to shoot him even if he was on the move, but I held off as I knew Jared was behind the bear hidden in the willows.

The first shot was supposed to be mine, but just as I prepared to fire, Jared shot.

The explanation I got later was he thought he couldn't miss, but I witnessed firsthand how he could.

The bear shifted gears and was at a dead run, headed west. He was a giant bear, a sight I will never forget. We had agreed beforehand that even if I had a marginal shot, I would still take it, as we would much rather deal with the collared bear in this more open terrain than in the dense willows of Dupuyer Creek.

Just before he entered the second willow patch, I took my shot at just over two hundred yards. I heard the bullet hit, and it sounded solid. The bear rolled, and then, to my surprise, was back up on his feet, entering the willows. The last thing I saw was him running up the creek bottom beyond the willows as if nothing had happened.

I was disgusted that our plan had not been followed. At that moment, the opportunity for an easy hunt ended; the bear was wounded. We met on the road, and Dave wasn't happy as I briefly explained what had happened.

The old road that led up the grassy hillside took us to a high point on the south side of the creek. From there, we hoped to locate the bear with telemetry. After driving to the top of the hill, I used my cell phone and got permission from the landowner to do some hunting. I told him several sheep had been killed, but I didn't say by what. If we couldn't get the bear that evening, we didn't want word to get out and have a bunch of helpers following us around the next day.

From the hilltop, we walked northwest. The grass was tall, so we avoided driving off the trail with the pickup and leaving tracks. I approached the edge, rifle in hand. This time, Jared carried a shotgun, and Dave had the telemetry.

We walked a short distance to where we could see the creek bottom and attempted to get the bear's location. The creek was visible for over thirty miles to where it exited the Rocky Mountains. Being so open, the line-of-sight capabilities of the telemetry should have immediately picked up the signal. However, the bear was not there.

I remembered a deep coulee that ran east of us into the creek and suggested the bear might have gone there. It was close, but a ridge blocked our line of sight, preventing us from receiving the telemetry signal. A collared animal could be one hundred yards away, but the signal would be unattainable if an obstacle was in the way; the collar had to be in the line of sight.

We then walked north and east. It was quite a ways farther than I thought. When we finally arrived at a point to look down into the bottom of the steep-sided coulee, the signal came in loud and clear. The bear was two hundred yards below us in the dense, brushy bottom. Two drainages in front of us and to our right dropped off the ridge to form the main coulee. At the point where they intersected were thick willows and cottonwood trees. That was where the signal came from. Below was a narrow bottom with rocks and chokecherries. The vegetation was less dense than above, and the grassy canyon walls were steep, sloping on both sides.

My first thought was not, *I'm glad we found him*, but rather, *Damn, I only brought three bullets.* I hadn't expected we'd find the bear when we left the pickup, as we speculated that he likely had followed the creek west. I didn't know it then, but Jarad had only brought three cartridges as well.

Now, we needed to make a decision.

"I only brought the three shells," I whispered to Dave. "If I walk back to the pickup, he might leave."

Without taking his eyes off the stand of trees, Dave replied, "You should be able to kill him with three shots."

Knowing it wasn't the wisest decision, I agreed to continue our bear hunt.

I carefully walked down the steep grassy slope of the coulee where the bear was held up. I positioned myself about forty yards up from the bottom and sat on an open side hill with a good view of the coulee. Settled into place, I lowered and adjusted the bipod on my rifle.

This time, the plan involved Jared approaching the bear from above. He would walk down into the forks of the coulee and scare the bear toward me. I worried Dahlie might attack Jarad. With the thick vegetation, I couldn't see that far up the coulee, and if something happened, it would be impossible to help him in time.

I watched Jared sneak down the ridge between the forks and disappear into the willows.

Suddenly, branches started breaking, followed by a loud roar, a sound scarier than any I had ever heard. A shot rang out; brush, willow, and tree branches broke and snapped as I saw the bear running toward me.

Jared had missed.

When bears run, their bodies move up and down. This bear was also moving side to side, skillfully dodging rocks as it hurried in my direction. When the running grizzly was one hundred fifty yards away, I discovered my bipod to be more of a hindrance than a help. It made it difficult to track my rifle with the bear's motion. Looking through my scope, I focused on the massive bear drawing closer by the second.

Just as I squeezed off a shot, the bear's front end went down. I missed, the bullet landing right over its back. I could always tell, after pulling the trigger, roughly where the bullet hit.

That was shell number one.

At one hundred yards, I fired again, hitting to the left as he swiftly dodged some rocks on his right.

There went shell number two.

With only one bullet left, I knew I had to make it count. The world slowed around me.

I knew the wounded bear was in good enough shape to kill us if I didn't finish this.

By now, the huge grizzly was only fifty yards away. If the bear didn't notice me on the sidehill, I decided to take my last shot after it ran past. That would be easier and safer than shooting at something on the run as it passed.

From the corner of my eye, I saw Jared running along the ridge opposite me. The sound of his shotgun reverberated throughout the coulee. The bear tumbled forward and started biting at his hip where Jared's slug had left a ten-inch gash.

I remembered then that while captured in my snare, this grizzly had been the meanest bear I had ever caught. Now, it was twice wounded, and here I sat with one last shell in my rifle.

The chokecherries below me were fifty feet across and not very dense; he stopped there, forty yards away. I watched him angrily spin circles and bite at his hip. I peered through my scope and prepared to take my last shot, knowing his attempt to run from us was over.

The bipod was of great help then, and the rifle steadied.

While the bear circled, I resisted the temptation to shoot. "Wait until he stops," I told myself. Then, suddenly, the grizzly stopped spinning and glared up the hill at Jared.

Through an opening in the chokecherries, I could make out his hump and see part of his chest. When I shot, it felt good. The bear let out a roar, circled once, stood up, and looked directly at me.

I will never know how he knew I was there; maybe he had heard the shot. I was focused and frozen in time.

That was my last bullet, and I found myself wondering if the pepper spray on my belt would stop a wounded grizzly. It would have to be that or use my rifle as a club.

Neither were good options.

We stared at each other for a moment, and then the bear went down. I could only see a portion of his body through the vegetation.

Jared stopped on the other side of the coulee directly across from me. He couldn't see the bear from his location. I held up my hand for him to wait and sat there to see what would happen next.

After a few minutes, Dave called from the top of the ridge, asking if the bear was dead. I responded that I couldn't see any movement. He then joined me, and we cautiously approached the bear, throwing small rocks toward him as we proceeded.

The bear didn't respond.

It was dead.

My final shot had hit its mark precisely, just left of the hump toward the heart. A year older than when I had first captured him, the bear now weighed over five hundred pounds. Even though his pelt was molting, he was still a magnificent animal.

We discovered that my earlier running shot had penetrated his left hindquarters and missed the bone. As tough as those bears were, he could have healed from such an injury.

Now that it was over, I realized how wrong things could have gone. What if Jared had been attacked while walking through the willows into the forks? How difficult would it have been to get there in time, shoot the bear, and not hit Jared in the process? I doubted spray would have been enough.

The worst-case scenario, however, would have been to run out of shells and helplessly watch as Jared was mauled or killed.

Experiences like these are what nightmares were made of.

I learned yet another valuable lesson that day—carry plenty of ammunition. Also, emphasize to everyone the importance of sticking with the plan. I often think about what my life would have been like had things turned out differently.

I cleaned my bear rifle that night and hoped I would never have to shoot it again. And as it turned out, that was the case, and the rifle still sits in my gun safe to this day.

I remember thinking all those years ago that such a purchase had been a mistake. The money I spent at that time in my life with two small children could have been used elsewhere. Turned out, that weapon saved our lives. After that, it became the best rifle I ever owned.

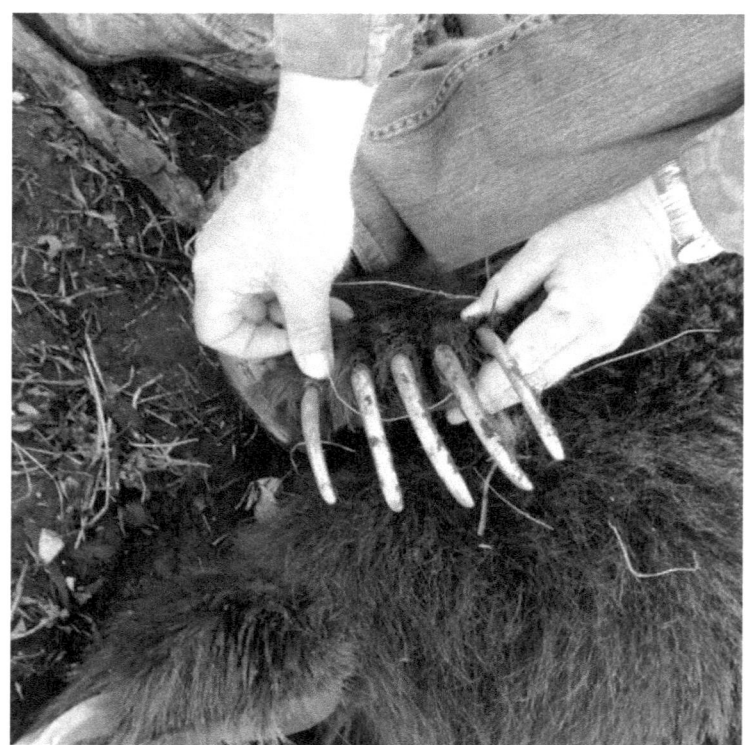

The enormous claws of a grizzly bear

A GAGGLE OF GRIZZLIES

CHAPTER 21

A Gaggle of Grizzlies

*"A rare gathering, a rare challenge—
many bears, one extraordinary day."*

After more than forty years, until the day I retired, I loved my job. It was always unpredictable, especially during grizzly bear season (spring through fall). It didn't matter if it was a weekend or a holiday. Whenever livestock were killed, I was there.

Setting equipment, the first night was always the best chance to capture the bear responsible. At some kill sites, it was a bear city by the second or third night, making it difficult to tell which was the culprit. That was why responding as quickly as possible was so important.

In 2010, I was a member of the Choteau Sheep Expo, a group of small sheep producers that got together every September to hold a sale. Rams and ewes of various breeds were displayed and sold for breeding stock. Weeks before the sale, I informed my supervisor that whatever happened, I would not be available on the first Saturday of September. I was committed to being at the sale, especially since I was the president.

I delivered the ram lambs I intended to sell the Friday evening before the sale. Being the one in charge, I had to make sure everything was set up and organized for the next day. Early Saturday morning (no surprise), my phone rang. A rancher told me a cow had been cornered in a fence and killed by a grizzly near Dupuyer. I called Steve, one of our veteran trappers who lived seventy-five miles away, and he said he would cover for me.

The sale went well, and when finished, I phoned Steve. He informed me that the rancher had seen a large boar grizzly and a sow with two cubs in the area before the kill. While there, he had time to put in only one pipe set at the kill site. He continued by saying he thought the boar was likely responsible for killing such a big cow. Happy he could help, I thanked him, and we made plans to meet in Dupuyer early in the morning.

That next day, we gathered at the trap site. Nothing had been captured, but it was clear that a bear, or bears, had returned and eaten on the carcass. The pipe set Steve had put in the day before remained untouched. It was too bad he hadn't had time to set up more equipment. I usually put in multiple snare sets whenever possible. The more equipment I had set, the better my chances, especially when dealing with a bear previously captured and relocated. They got smart; in all my years of trapping, I had never seen a bear caught twice in a pipe set. However, today, we had plenty of time and planned to do some serious bear trapping.

The kill site was in an open area, far from any trees or the nearby creek bottom, where the bears called home. It was clear how the older cow had been cornered in the fence and attacked.

The pen set that captured the sow

I was glad I brought extra snares, as it looked like more than one bear had been present.

With no trees nearby to construct a pen, we utilized thirty feet of four-foot-high, wooden slatted snow fence to encircle the cow's remains. The entrance was a three-foot opening with the side posts slanted outward on top, making it narrower at the bottom. A foot snare was set at the narrow base, and four hundred and fifty pounds of weights were attached with a chain.

I had used those specific weights for years; they came from an old mine scale in Nevada and were perfect for the purpose. The weights were fifty pounds each and had handles through which a chain ran and attached to the snare cable. They were smooth, without sharp edges that might fray the cable, and had witnessed countless bears being captured through the years.

Steve moved his original set closer to the cow, remembering not to have our sets too close together in case more than one bear was captured. If they could reach each other, they might fight. The rancher stopped by and offered to bring us some heavy tractor weights to use as anchors. We gladly accepted the offer, as it allowed us to set two more pipe sets. With four sets in place, we called it a day.

Driving home, I phoned Dave to update him on our progress. He planned to meet us in Dupuyer early the next morning.

Sleeping that night was difficult. After setting, I always worried if the safety latches on the throw-arms had been disabled, if the snares were far enough apart, and a hundred other things.

The following day, full of anticipation, I headed for Dupuyer. After meeting Dave and Steve, we drove three miles out of town to a high point where we could use binoculars to check our traps. Despite it still being somewhat dark, we could clearly see not one but *five* grizzly bears at the trap site!

This was going to be an interesting morning.

In the faint light, we watched a smaller bear walk around, and after a moment, we concluded that the other four were captured. How well the bears were caught remained to be seen. We knew it would be challenging to tranquilize and work five bears in close quarters. None of us had ever experienced anything like this before.

We were able to drive within thirty yards of the bears before a barbed wire fence separated us. Where the snow fence set had once been was a large older sow. The fence was in ruins, with broken slabs of wood lying on the ground. One yearling cub was caught in a pipe set twenty yards away. Not paying much attention to us and wandering around confused was a second yearling that had not been captured. In another pipe set was an enormous male, and close by in the last pipe set was another young medium-sized male. The bears were all vocalizing, agitated, and nervous. A sight and sound I will never forget.

First, we needed to determine how well they were captured. Using binoculars from inside the pickup, we scrutinized the traps. Fortunately, everything looked good. We had been lucky that this had happened in the open instead of on a brushy creek bottom.

Next, we determined the weight of the free-roaming cub. Dave prepared a tranquilizer dart accordingly. My supervisor, Greg, arrived. At the same time, the bear specialist's assistant showed up with another culvert trap to add to those we already had with us. We were glad for the help.

Once the tranquilizer gun was ready, Dave and I drove through a nearby gate and slowly made our way toward the uncaptured cub. The cub kept looking at its mother and seemed unaware of our presence. It preferred to stay close to its captured sibling rather than the sow, possibly because the sow was close to the large boar, and the cub knew to avoid him.

After a short time, Dave had a clear shot out the pickup window and launched the dart into the cub's hind quarter. Within minutes, the tranquilizer took effect. The cub wandered a short distance, staggered, and then fell asleep.

Now came the tricky part: walk in, grab the cub, and move far enough away to safely work it—all the while hoping one of the angry bears didn't escape its snare. That was when Steve, Greg, and Jared went to work.

Darting the captive bears

They covered our every move with their shotguns as we walked in to retrieve the cub. The sow was our greatest concern. It was obvious she wasn't happy watching us mess with her cub. Once the cub was laid on a tarp, we dragged it a safe distance away to be processed (ID ear tag, weighed, and measured).

Standing guard

Next was the sow, which was agitated, huffing, growling, and popping her jaws. This was due to the presence of the old boar and the concern for her cubs. Fortunately, all the bears were caught well, but to not run out of things to think about, I contemplated the possibility of equipment failure. I worried about a swivel breaking or something coming apart, releasing one of these angry bears.

Dave, carrying his dart gun, and I with my shotgun approached the sow from the south while Steve and Greg guarded us from the west. When we were close enough, Dave fired the dart, which hit precisely where he aimed. We stepped back and waited in the pickup for the drugs to take effect. The bear swiped at her foot several times, which, after what had happened in Choteau, made me pay a little more attention to this, before settling down and falling asleep.

We had recently started using a combination of Telazol and Medetomidine in the tranquilizer mix. The combination was heavy on Medetomidine, which had a reversal drug that would be injected after the bear was put into the culvert trap, allowing it to wake a short time later. Once the sow was unconscious, she was rolled onto a tarp and dragged several yards away. This took considerably more effort than the cub. She was processed and then slid into a culvert trap.

There was plenty of help, and more was on the way. Looking down the two-track trail, we spotted the Dupuyer school bus driving toward us with nine students and a teacher inside. As it came to a stop, I quickly ran over and told them they would have to wait on the bus until the last bear was tranquilized. The looks on their faces as they watched those bears were priceless. What an incredible opportunity for these kids, one I'm sure they will remember for the rest of their lives. Not many classrooms had the chance to go on such an unforgettable field trip!

Next to be darted was the old boar. Once again, we walked in, tranquilized, and processed the bear. He was then transferred into a culvert trap like the others. All that remained was the three-year-old boar and the cub. Two darts were prepared; it was getting late, so they were darted simultaneously. I was concerned that processing two bears at once would take some time, and the second might wake up. As the kids exited the bus, I said, "If we tell you, be prepared to hurry back on."

The yearling could be worked quickly and was processed first (no collar would be used). When we finished, it was placed into a culvert trap. Now, all that remained was the three-year-old.

We worked quickly, measuring, tattooing, and inserting a PIT tag. Telazol was a safe and reliable drug, but the downside was if used alone, it would take several hours for a bear to fully recover. On the other hand, Medetomidine had a quicker recovery and a reversal option. However, stimulation could sometimes cause this recovery to be spontaneous.

What happened next taught us to go a little heavier on the Telazol in the future.

The voluntary recovery happened suddenly, just as we prepared to put the three-year-old in the culvert. Three people were on each side, ready to lift and slide him into the culvert when he awoke. The bear opened his eyes, raised his head, and sleepily looked around. Steve was guarding us with his shotgun, and we all wondered what to do next. Then, the three-hundred-pound male emitted a low growl and struggled to get up while the teacher hurriedly ushered the kids back onto the bus.

The bear was to be moved only a short distance and released since we felt it was not involved in the cattle depredation. It was already processed and partially sedated, so I strongly suggested we let it go and do an on-site release, figuring we would have time to run to the safety of our pickups. It would be best to do that before the bear fully recovered. A decision needed to be made quickly since the bear was confused and on the verge of fully awakening.

While I straddled the top of the bear, without warning, Dave appeared from behind me with a syringe in hand. He gave the bear a shot in the neck, where there was minimal fat. We all breathed a sigh of relief as the bear relaxed and went back to sleep. Steve, who always had a sense of humor, later joked that he had hoped to see me ride that bear across the prairie. Considering the position I was in, that actually might have happened.

We loaded the last bear and headed toward Choteau. At Dave's house, we watered the bears and made phone calls to find relocation sites. It was a seven-and-a-half-hour ordeal.

I never heard that any of these bears ever caused problems after that. We suspected the old boar was responsible for the depredation but couldn't say for sure.

I look back on that day—on my whole career—and think about how fortunate we were not to have been involved in a disaster. To my knowledge, five grizzlies had never been captured and processed at one time, in one location before or since.

The convoy of culvert traps

Bear caught in a snare with the free-ranging yearling

Captured yearling with sibling

CHAPTER 22

The Scariest Wolf Calling Experience Ever!

*"Every sound in the wild has consequences—
sometimes terrifying ones."*

After reintroduction into Montana and Idaho in the mid-nineties and natural migration from Canada, wolf numbers increased in my district every year. By 2012, there was a healthy population of wolves along the East Front of the Rockies. I had a busy spring that year, with more work than I could handle. Early that summer, I spent three days in Kalispell, flying in the helicopter to help one of my co-workers, Ted.

Ted had three packs of wolves simultaneously killing livestock. Luckily, they each had a collared member and could be located with telemetry. The morning the helicopter picked me up from my house, it was beautiful. We flew west through the Rocky Mountains south of Glacier National Park. Below us were forests of pine and quaking aspen; lush green filled the space in between. Towering rock mountainsides with cascading waterfalls rose toward the sky as we made our way west. It's little wonder that people come from all over the world to see this place.

When we started hunting, we discovered that the place where these three packs called home was thick with trees and underbrush, a far cry from the open country on the east side of the mountains. This was going to be a challenge.

Of the three packs, we helped Ted with only one. The other two resided in such rough tree-covered terrain that we occasionally got a glimpse of a wolf and nothing more. When we were done, I told Tim that Ted could have this place. Besides, I had wolves of my own causing problems that needed attention back home.

The pack I was dealing with consisted of seventeen members with many hungry mouths to feed. While deer and elk were plentiful, cattle remained their prey of choice. These wolves were uncollared, so I spent the next week working with Brad, the FWP wolf specialist.

On four-wheelers, we traveled to a trap site along an old trail that ran north and south at the base of the mountainfront and set a trap line. The trail consisted of aspen and pine trees, open grassy areas, and creek bottoms.

Besides wolves, the mountainfront was perfect for one other animal—grizzly bears.

Sitting astride a four-wheeler was not the best place to be if an angry sow charged out of the trees to defend her trapped cub.

The trapline ran four miles, and the lack of wind during our eight days of trapping was a blessing. At each location, we stopped our four-wheelers a distance away to listen for signs of a trapped cub. If we heard nothing, we'd cautiously approached the set.

On the eighth day, Brad had other business to attend to, so the rancher accompanied me. Stopping at the base of a pine-covered hillside, we shut off our four-wheelers and heard the unmistakable howl of a wolf at our next trap site. After exchanging looks, the rancher and I drove to the top of the hill where we found a young gray male of about fifty pounds waiting for us in the set.

The wolf watched intently as I prepared the drug and then approached to place the catchpole around its neck. The noose was tightened just enough to control but not choke him. After pulling the loop closed, the rancher held on tight as I hand-injected the sedative. The tracking collar was placed, and we left the wolf in the shade to wake up later and be on its way.

Our trapline was pulled, and in the following days, the calf killing continued. However, with the help of the helicopter and our new collared wolf, we reduced the size of the pack, but many remained.

Two weeks passed, and one morning, I heard the collared wolf's signal on a brushy creek bottom at the base of the mountains. I knew other wolves were likely with the collar, so I decided to try calling them in to get this calf killing stopped.

After parking my pickup and walking a half mile, I reached a low brim that ran east and west on the north side of the creek. In front of me was a vast meadow filled with tall grass and willows nestled against a pine-covered hillside. A half mile to the right was the base of the Rocky Mountains. Amongst the thick willows before me were small openings where I hoped a lured wolf would appear.

Dressed in camouflage, I found a comfortable spot and sat against a tree. I had with me an electronic call, my 25-06 rifle, binoculars, and bear pepper spray.

After settling in, I began to call by mimicking the howl of a young wolf. After howling several times, I waited. In one of the openings, a wolf suddenly appeared. It was two hundred yards away, a relatively easy shot. However, with it standing in the tall grass, I couldn't tell if the wolf wore a collar. The last thing I wanted to do was accidentally shoot my collared wolf. This wolf was the same medium gray as the collared one, so I decided not to take the chance.

Instead of coming in my direction, the wolf slunk north into the willows and disappeared. I hoped it would continue and appear where the willows ended on my right. A moment later, the large wolf came into view, one hundred fifty yards away. Looking through the scope, I saw it wore no collar and shot. The wolf fell to the ground, never realizing what had happened.

I knew the collared wolf, and possibly more, were still in the willows. After my shot, I waited ten minutes for things to calm down. I planned to call for another forty-five minutes. Wolves, even though close, sometimes approached slowly.

I howled periodically for almost an hour with no response.

I was sure the wolves were still there.

Going against that little voice in my head (that had been right so many times in the past) emphatically telling me, "No!" I decided to call one last time by imitating a mouse squeak. I was always reluctant to use a distress sound where there might be bears.

And if any place looked like bear habitat, I was staring at it right in front of me.

After playing the high-pitched mouse squeak for ten seconds, I turned it off and waited. If the wolves were around and interested, that should be enough to coax them in. After five minutes, I took my binoculars and decided to scan the openings one last time. The base of the willows was heavily shaded, and a wolf standing there might not easily be seen with the naked eye.

I slowly began searching from left to right until my binoculars landed on an open clearing.

An old, ratty-looking sow grizzly with a collar lumbered toward me some fifty yards away. Through my binoculars, she appeared much closer than she actually was.

My heart raced as I thought how foolish I was to get into this predicament. The bear was close, and to make matters worse, she had a yearling cub at her heels. I knew I couldn't let the bear get any closer, so I stood. Upon spotting me at thirty yards, the old sow stopped and stood on her hind legs.

We stared at each other as I thought about what to do next. After a moment, I cautiously began to back away, intently watching to see what she would do next.

At the edge of the brim, I turned to leave and went down out of sight. Walking fast, I looked over my shoulder, praying that she wouldn't come charging over the ridge behind me. I kept on watching as I walked toward the pickup. I had pepper spray, but it wasn't an option with the wind blowing toward me. I knew that if she charged, my only defense would be my rifle.

The farther I walked, the more open it became. I was relieved when I finally reached the pickup, but then suddenly remembered that my electronic call and binoculars were still at the calling stand. I had no desire to walk back in there, but if I was careful, I thought I could drive the pickup to where they were.

After slowly approaching the top of the brim, I drove alongside my equipment. The bears were still there, some thirty yards away. I thought they would run once they saw my vehicle, but the pair didn't budge. The mother bear watched me while the cub remained unconcerned, digging for something behind her. Several minutes passed, and they showed no signs of leaving. I slowly opened my door, ready to get back in if necessary, and grabbed the call and binoculars. Once I was safely back in the pickup, I closed the door and drove off with a sigh of relief. I then retrieved the wolf shot earlier, a large yearling male.

Bears, like people, come with different personalities. That day, it was my good fortune to encounter a sow that was not aggressive. After this scary experience, I was wiser when calling wolves in bear country.

It's incredible how many ways there are to obtain an education, and mine continued until the day I retired. That was not the first time I had learned a lesson the hard way, nor would it be my last.

A sow with small cubs near Dupuyer Creek

CHAPTER 23

The Killer Wolves of Looking Glass

"Wolves don't care about boundaries. My job was to help people determined to protect what's theirs."

Mike and rancher with the goat-killing wolf

The phone rang.

It was Stan, the bear manager on the Reservation.

Time for an adventure.

Stan explained that a livestock producer north of town had shot a wolf feeding on a goat that morning. He said the wolf had been alone, and I hoped he was right. Experience, however, taught me that was usually not the case. I loaded my equipment and headed north.

Stan's main job was working with bears. But as time passed, wolves became an increasing part of our workload. After meeting Stan, we drove fifteen miles to the ranch to learn more from the producer. He explained that the goat had belonged to his wife and was the only one they owned. I was happy to hear this, thinking we might be done since there were no others.

But the rancher had cows and small calves in the pasture that surrounded the house, which concerned me. We were told that their son-in-law was the one who had shot the wolf near his home a quarter mile away.

The ranch sat at the base of the Rocky Mountains, close to Glacier National Park. It was a beautiful area, especially in June. Stunning green grass and flowers unfurled before majestic snow-covered mountains. But it could be a brutal place in the winter with below-zero weather and wind.

We proceeded to the son-in-law's residence. Like many of those homes, it sat in the open with no trees. Two hundred yards from the house lay the wolf. It was a large gray, approximately ninety pounds. The mass and power of these animals never ceased to amaze me. Nearby were the remains of a large goat, two-thirds consumed. It was evident by the amount eaten that more than one wolf had been responsible.

I met the son-in-law and gave him a hearty congratulations as it was rare for a producer to have a gun that was sighted in, remain calm, and be a good enough shot to do what he had. Even though it was early summer, Stan told the producer to come to the office, and he would issue a permit for him to keep the hide.

After examining the wolf and goat, I suggested we look around the pasture containing the cows and calves for kills. I also needed to search for tracks that might show how many wolves we were dealing with. Northwest of the kill site was a coulee bottom that ran east and west. There, we found two small calves freshly killed the night before by wolves. Both were less than half consumed. The cooperator then told us he had found a dead calf on the west end two days earlier and, at the time, had assumed it died naturally and was then fed on by coyotes.

We proceeded to that location and found the remains of not one but *three* calves. They had been killed a few days earlier, and little remained. Searching the area, we saw wolf scat, and on the hides were canine tooth punctures consistent with the spacing of a wolf. Five calves—I knew then that our work was far from over.

There was nowhere to move the cattle, so I could not set equipment at the kill site. Also, I worried about catching a bear around the dead calves and planned to return with a four-wheeler the following day to determine where the wolves were coming from. They wouldn't stop killing on their own; they never did.

I pulled into the ranch early the next morning. The producer and his wife greeted me, utterly distraught. The previous night, the wolves had returned, killing two more calves close to their house. Examining the calves, I discovered very little had been eaten.

When I turned toward them, I found the couple watching me, stress lining their faces. They were not young, but not old either. They were just hard-working people trying to make a living on land that had been owned by their people for countless generations. In all my years performing the job, all of the livestock kills I had examined, the different predators I had dealt with, and the many cooperators I'd worked with, I had never seen more anguish and fear in people's faces as I witnessed that morning.

"Can you bring in a helicopter?" the rancher asked.

"I could, but your share would be about $500 an hour," I replied.

The couple didn't respond.

"First, we need to capture and place a radio-transmitting collar on one of the wolves to locate the pack." I shook my head. "Without the collar, it'll be like looking for a needle in a haystack. Getting a helicopter before collaring a wolf would be a waste of your money."

After a moment of silence, the husband slowly replied, "We don't care; we had seven calves killed near the house. What will the wolves do when we turn the cattle into the far pastures?"

Mike searching for wolf sign on location

They had cows and leased pasture for other people's cattle every summer, which was a big part of their income.

"Who'll want to bring their cows here with the wolves killing everything?"

They lived simply, and this was their livelihood. Because of the wolves, they could lose everything. Never in my life had I come up against anything quite like this.

"Okay, give me a few days," I finally said. "I'm going to use the four-wheeler to search the trails, creek crossing, every square inch in between to figure out where the wolves are coming from. But it's going to take some time." I felt bad for them.

After our visit, I took the four-wheeler north. A highway bordered the ranch to the south, so the wolves probably weren't coming from that direction. The ranch was covered with lush green grass this time of year. My only chance of finding tracks was on the cow trails or in the mud.

I found old wolf tracks in dried mud. Most of the tracks led north and south. Unfortunately, there were just as many grizzly tracks. The problem with wolves, as opposed to coyotes, was that they often traveled long distances to kill from where they lived. The farthest example I witnessed of this was a wolf I captured at a kill site eight and a half miles from where it called home. The GPS collars we installed were invaluable.

Two long days were spent on the four-wheeler, scouring the area for tracks. On the second day, I stopped near a large rock on a hillside and sat down to eat lunch. Halfway through my sandwich, I looked to the west. As if they had magically appeared were the Rocky Mountain Front and Two-Medicine Lake.

Time stopped.

I held my sandwich and stared, realizing how much I took for granted. Living in such a beautiful place and seeing it every day, I sometimes forgot how blessed I was to have such a life.

Stan had been busy with bears, so we met at the ranch on the third morning. I told him I thought the wolves were coming from the north. We planned to find a high spot and howl, then either call them in or, at the very least, spot them with binoculars and see where they were coming from. We could see in the open areas between the trees two to three miles north and west of our first location. The thick, quaking aspen to the east and all the grizzlies living there made me nervous about calling.

The two grizzly-infested creek bottoms a short distance below us made matters worse.

All I planned to do was howl, but I knew from experience there was no guarantee a grizzly wouldn't step out to see what the wolves were up to.

I howled, we glassed, and I howled again fifteen minutes later. It was a beautiful morning with sunshine and no wind. Should a wolf appear, we would spot it, reflecting in the green grass.

We sat for an hour with no wolves and no answering howls. We would try again further north.

The following location was a mile away on another high point. Again, after sitting for an hour, we came up with the same results. Stan then told me the ridge to the north would be ideal. "From the top," he explained, "you can look north into that wide basin along the base of the mountains—Kiowa Camp." Although it was seven miles from the kill site, it was a distance they could easily travel.

We proceeded north. The country was open grassland until three hundred yards before the ridge where the trees started. We parked our four-wheelers in a depression and then hiked through the thick trees toward the top. I took the electronic call and a shotgun in case of a bear encounter. We both carried bear spray, which, on this particular day with little wind, might work should a bear appear.

Entering the trees, I found the forest dense and dark. We walked to a place where we could look north into the basin and sat on a fallen log. There was very little visibility from our vantage point, as there was nothing but aspens and pine trees for miles. Hopefully, we would hear them answer if they were there.

I started the call with two long, mournful wolf howls. Before the second howl finished, the wolves began howling back, not in the basin below but seventy-five yards away from us in the thick trees!

We had found the rendezvous site!

Finding this location was more than half the battle; now, we needed to plan what to do next. Had the wind been coming from the right direction, they could have appeared to us then and there. As it was, the breeze was blowing from us to them. I didn't howl again; they already knew we were there. I sat intently watching with my shotgun ready for over thirty minutes in case they showed. Nothing appeared.

Thirty minutes after finding the wolves' location, we silently left and returned to Browning. Using GPS coordinates, we found the tree ridge on Google Earth. Scrolling up and down, it was as if we were looking down from a helicopter.

We discovered an open coulee bottom in the trees that ran two hundred yards north and south, a short distance east of the wolves' location. Depending on the wind, it would be an ideal place to call from the next morning. A light breeze was predicted from the west the following day, which would be perfect.

Early the next morning, we approached from the east and drove the pickup within a half mile of our destination. Silently, we walked west toward the open draw we'd discovered and reached our call stand. I was excited, but also worried at the chance of accidentally calling a grizzly.

Once we arrived at a point of trees on the southeast corner, I noticed we didn't have a clear view of the entire draw to our right. It curved, and there were only seventy yards of visibility looking in that direction. The breeze was blowing from the southwest. I could picture a wolf circling to catch our scent once we started calling. I asked Stan if he wouldn't mind going to the far end of the draw in case that should happen. He headed in that direction.

I had a shotgun, 25-06 rifle, and bear spray ready as I took my position to begin calling. I gave Stan a few minutes to get into place as I couldn't see him from my location. The conditions were ideal, and I sat there, hoping the wolves were still around and would come to the call.

During this time, the Tribe only allowed wildlife managers to trap or call wolves. Because of this, we had a better chance of success since the pack was less educated about our methods than the wolves to the south.

I began the electronic call with a couple of howls and intently watched the other side of the draw, expecting the wolves to appear. If they were there, it would happen quickly. The trees were one hundred yards away; it would be close if they did show up.

In less than a minute, I heard the blast of Stan's shotgun! He had a semi-automatic, and having taken only one shot, I took that as a good sign. Even though Stan had shot, I waited a few minutes and resumed calling. All the time, I worried that a bear would appear from the trees behind me.

In fact, many believed the sound of a gunshot attracted particular bears who were used to eating gut piles during hunting season. I called intermittently for another forty-five minutes; nothing appeared. I arose and walked down the draw toward Stan. As I approached, I spotted a large gray wolf lying twenty yards from him. As we had speculated earlier, it had circled downwind to smell me, but Stan had been in the right place at the right time.

From the tracks we found and the howling we had heard the day before, we decided the pack was small.

So we began setting equipment to capture what remained. We placed three foot snares and two traps. Select-A-Catch foot snares were preferred as most bears, if accidentally caught, could pull hard enough to break the connection and be released. After the traps were set, we planned to return early in the morning, check the equipment, and call again.

The next day as we bumped along through the dense aspens, we saw several piles of bear scat, a reminder of the danger of the job. We parked in the exact location as the day before and walked to the same calling stand. The conditions were once again favorable. I took my seat against a tree, and Stan settled down in the draw where he had previously been successful.

The vegetation and brush behind me and all the grizzlies that might be lurking there still made me nervous. The best thing was to try to block that fear from my mind, but in the same respect, be vigilant and ready should something happen.

I turned on the call, letting loose three howls. The wolves immediately answered close, before me and to the left. Soon, they appeared, four eerie, gray ghosts in the early morning light.

Waiting for wolves at the call site

Instead of coming toward me, however, they walked sideways on the opposite side of the draw, heading north. The low brush they walked through yielded to a solid wall of aspens and vegetation. If they entered there, they would disappear. It would be good to get more than one, as I knew once I shot, the remainder would never respond to that particular call again. Here was my opportunity to help get the calf killing stopped.

Suddenly, the wolves paused and looked in my direction as if they knew I was there. I peered through the scope, placing the wolf closest to the trees in the crosshairs. I squeezed the trigger, and it fell. I hoped the other three might turn around back into the open. Instead, they ran for the safety of the trees. I chambered another round, put the last running wolf in my scope, and shot but could not see the results as it entered the dense foliage.

    I sat there for a few minutes before I saw Stan coming up the draw toward me. After explaining what had happened, we walked to the first yearling wolf that had fallen in its tracks. Several yards away, we found the second wolf. I was more than surprised that I had shot him on the run. We then checked our equipment and found nothing had been captured the night before. After setting two more traps in the draw where we had just called, we headed home.

    The following day, the wind was blowing hard, as it often did in this country, so it was no use trying to call. With anticipation, we drove in to check our equipment. We first visited the traps placed the day earlier in the draw.

    Rounding the corner where Stan had shot the first wolf, we were relieved to find the other two wolves had been captured. From the sign we had seen earlier, perhaps one wolf remained. We reset and continued to check the rest of the line, but no other wolves were caught.

    I met Stan the following day, and we arrived early at the trap site. This location was eighty miles from my home, one hundred sixty miles roundtrip. Having five counties under my jurisdiction, I not only dealt with wolves but grizzly and coyote problems as well, and sometimes found it overwhelming. I wanted to wrap this up as I had many other problems to deal with.

    We checked our equipment and finally came to the last set, a Select-A-Catch foot snare. The trees were thick, and the trail was narrow. The snare was placed where two paths intersected.

    I noticed one of the fir trees at the trap site had a broken branch. Several pine trees were bunched together where the foot snare was located, making it hard to see. Studying the broken limbs, I told Stan, "We must have caught something." But I detected no movement. Maybe whatever it was had escaped.

    Stan exited the pickup and took a couple of steps forward. Peering into the thick trees, he exclaimed, "We've got a big wolf!" He grabbed the shotgun; this was the last one, and we were finished. The wolf was the large alpha male, which was more than likely the instigator. Wrapping this up was a relief not only for Stan and me but for the ranchers as well.

Gratitude was not a strong enough word to describe how the ranchers felt toward us. The sense of purpose that overcame me that day was yet another defining moment in my career. It reminded me how vitally important our program was to the people whose livelihoods depended on us.

Although wolves were always present, it wasn't until a decade later that more calves were killed. Stan and I were retired by then and happy to let someone else be responsible for tracking them down.

CHAPTER 24

Lions Stalking the Bed & Breakfast

"Lions at the door, the wild had claimed the night."

Driving home from the Sweet Grass Hills one July afternoon, I received a call from Steve, our wildlife specialist, to the south. He asked if I had my night-vision rifle handy. I wasn't sure what he had going on, but I was glad it wasn't *Stan* asking me that question.

Although Steve usually started conversations with a joke, he was serious this time. "A lady south of Great Falls who owns a bed and breakfast just called. She says her security cameras caught two mountain lions hanging around the place. One was huge, the other smaller. They've been chasing her horses, hunting her house cats. They killed two deer within twenty yards of the front door. Neighbors have been complaining about these lions for over a month."

"That's not good," I replied. Their biggest concern was the safety of their guests. No one was currently staying at the bed and breakfast, but they had people coming the following week and were very worried.

"Fish & Wildlife and Parks gave me permission to remove the lions," Steve went on. There was a long pause as he thought. "I could shoot them from the B&B's second-story deck. Just need your rifle, Mike."

Of course, I agreed.

The B&B sat atop a hillside overlooking the Missouri River. The location was an ideal habitat for many wildlife species, such as the small herd of deer that stayed close to the buildings. Undoubtedly, the deer were the reason the lions were there.

When Steve called, I was one hundred miles away. Being recently divorced and with little else to do that evening, I volunteered to help. Steve called the owners, who were happy we were coming. They told him we could spend the night and wanted to fix us supper.

After meeting Steve that afternoon, we drove up the windy gravel road through steep pine-covered hills. I couldn't help but think about how hard it would be to get into this place in the winter. As we pulled into the yard, we saw a horse corral that held the five horses the lions had chased. These were rescue horses and were never ridden. The couple also had a couple dozen cats and a dog. Twenty tame deer lived close to the house. Some people fed wildlife, which was against the law, but when Steve questioned the couple, they said they were not feeding them and told him the deer only came in sometimes to eat hay with the horses.

The B&B was a two-story building with an upper deck surrounded by tall ponderosa pines. The location was within a subdivision of homes on twenty-acre lots. Looking around, I realized I couldn't use my night-vision rifle as several nearby houses surrounded their property. Shotguns would be our only option.

The owner, Kevin, who was dressed like he was on a Hawaiian vacation, met us as we got out of our pickup. He explained, "Our cameras around the buildings captured footage of two lions hanging around. They've been here for the past four nights."

We followed him a short distance into a large patch of chokecherry bushes near the house. There, he showed us the two deer the lions had killed. One kill was fresh from the night before. The other, fifteen yards away, was a couple of days older. The kills along with the video evidence had me feeling like we had a good chance of solving the problem that night.

We surveyed the area and devised a plan. Steve retrieved one deer carcass and placed it fifty feet from the house below the yard light. He then installed a battery-powered motion detector to alert us inside when the lions approached. I removed three Select-A-Catch foot snares from my pickup, thinking this would be an ideal location to set.

The first snare was placed in a cubby. I took the freshest deer carcass and put sticks and branches on both sides in a V shape. The bait was placed in the narrow part of the V. I then set the foot snare in the open end and put rocks and sticks around it to force the lion to place its foot into the snare circle. I next camouflaged the set with a dusting of dirt and then anchored the snare to the thick trunk of a chokecherry.

A short distance away, another foot snare was set on a well-defined trail. I placed four-inch-diameter logs on each side of the loop to force the lion to step between them to activate the snare as it walked down the trail. When stepped on, the cable would slide up the four vertical wires that held the snare in place. The loop would then pull sideways to cinch around the animal's wrist.

After completing this set, I noticed a large pile of logs nearby. This was close to the deer kill where Steve had placed the motion detector. In front of those neatly stacked log ends ran another trail. I put my last Select-A-Catch there as well.

The set was almost completed when Kevin came over to see how I was faring. As he watched, I could see he had doubts about my methods. Finally, he said, "I still have a bunch of house cats around and wouldn't like to see any of them caught.

I chuckled. "The snare base has a tension device that takes a certain amount of weight to activate. A house cat's too light to trigger it."

"Well, what about the deer? They come in all the time."

"That shouldn't be a problem. The chain here is too long to close tightly around most deer legs. But if we do catch one, we'll just let it go."

The B&B owners were animal lovers, and I was glad he asked me questions so I could explain how selective and humane the device was.

"You know I have a yellow lab," he said finally. "I'll keep a close eye on him, but what happens if he gets caught?"

At that, I balled my fist and pushed down on the pan of my recently completed set; the snare jumped up, tightening the chain around my wrist. "Then we will just let him go," I replied as I took it off. The look on his face was priceless.

The foot snares and motion detectors were in place. When we finished, we went into the house for supper. There, April, Kevin's wife, served a fabulous meal. I hadn't been getting too many of those lately cooking for myself, and it was greatly appreciated.

I enjoyed that evening. Kevin and April loved animals— though they definitely loved their horses, cats, and deer more than the lions. There was also the liability issue to consider should something happen to one of their guests. I learned, to my surprise, that April even liked spiders. When Kevin said he needed to knock down a web in front of one of the cameras, she practically became unglued. It was an entertaining evening, that was for sure.

After we ate, Steve and I got to work. According to the videos, the lions had been coming in around midnight. We took our shotguns to the living room on the top floor. A sliding-glass door opened to a railed deck facing the chokecherries and the yard light where we expected the lions to appear. There were several potted plants and a lot of junk on the deck. We cleared the area of obstacles and took one last look around before dark. There was not much else to do now but wait.

We seated ourselves in the large living room. Two TVs hung on the wall, monitoring different outside locations. We then had an enjoyable visit with our hosts. Even though Kevin had spent his younger years in Montana, he had left for a while, and the life he had led afterward made him the man he was today. April was from the same mold; they both resembled ex-flower children and made a perfect couple.

Soon after dark, the TV monitor showing the east side (two hours earlier than expected) captured the image of one of the largest lions I had ever seen prowling toward the first deer carcass. At that moment, one of the motion detectors Steve had set loudly started broadcasting, "Activity: station one," and kept repeating it. Hearing the noise from within the house, the lion ran past the deer carcass and entered the chokecherries. Steve and I grabbed our shotguns and went out on the deck.

Steve had a flashlight taped to the barrel of his shotgun. Studying the chokecherries away from the yard light was dark, I saw nothing. Since Steve was looking directly behind the light on his shotgun, he whispered to me he could see the reflection of the lion's green eyes but not the body. It wasn't far away, and I whispered he should shoot it in the head. He fired, and we immediately heard the lion thrashing below us.

We hurried down the stairs, out the door, and into the chokecherries, shining our flashlights where we had last seen it. There, we discovered one of the largest lions I had ever seen. A one hundred sixty-pound male, over eight feet long, including his tail.

Although relieved it was dead, April was upset and so went over to the lion, placed both hands on it, and prayed.

Knowing our work was only half done, we once again took up our positions in front of the monitors inside. It took thirty minutes for the second lion to appear. It came from the same direction as the first. In all the excitement, Steve had forgotten to disconnect the motion alarm after shooting the first lion. Again, a loud voice announced, "Activity: station one."

We slid the glass door open in time to see the lion loping away below us in the yardlight. Had it sensed the dead lion nearby? Heard the motion detector or the glass door sliding open? Perhaps all of the above. One thing was for sure: the lion was gone. We had missed our chance.

Steve disconnected the sensor, and we planned for him to sit outside on the deck. From the inside, watching the monitors, we would alert him by knocking lightly on the glass if we saw the lion return. While we were on the deck rearranging the flowerpots, we heard a sudden noise that sounded like branches rattling and a scuffling sound.

Steve exclaimed, "I think we have it in a snare!"

No way, I thought. We had just seen it run off.

Steve and I took our shotguns and flashlights downstairs to investigate. Cautiously, we walked into the chokecherry patch, shining our lights toward the sets. Two large green eyes stared in our direction. Steve raised his shotgun and fired.

How could that lion have gotten in the snare so fast?

However it happened, she was caught in the cubby set where I had used the deer as bait. The old female wasn't nearly as big as the first but was ancient and had brown teeth worn to the gums. April approached the dead lion, laid her hands on it, and said another prayer.

Our work was done; it was time for bed. April showed us to our rooms on the bottom floor. I had no trouble falling asleep but woke a while later with the events of that evening running through my mind.

The next thing I knew, April was running down the hall crying, "Guys, guys, get up! There's another cougar, and I think it's in one of your traps!"

Steve and I jumped from our beds and hurriedly got dressed. We didn't know what to think now. We had studied the videos; there had only been *two* lions. April told us in the kitchen that when she had let the dog out, it had started barking. She had walked outside to investigate, and that's when she saw the lion.

It was just starting to get daylight. Everything was black and white with limited visibility. Steve and I stepped outside and cautiously walked toward the snares, shotguns ready, as April watched from the doorway.

The first set we approached was where the female had been caught the night before.

The second, a short distance away, was still in place, empty.

Unless she had been seeing things, it had to be in the third set by the pile of logs. But there was no lion. *What's going on here?* I asked myself. As we drew closer, I noticed the ground had been scuffed up, but nothing else seemed out of the ordinary.

"He must have gotten out," Steve whispered from behind me.

"Looks like it," I replied.

Inching forward in the dim light, I discovered the snare cable led into an opening in the logs. I ducked my head to peer inside—and came face-to-face with the eyes of a lion not six feet from me.

"Nope, still here!" I told Steve as I stepped back, raised my shotgun, and fired.

It was another male. We concluded that the old female must have been in heat. That would explain her being accompanied by the two toms. The last lion had been the one we had seen running away earlier. It was a fair-sized male but smaller than the first. *Now*, we were done!

Steve and I went on many adventures, but the hunt at the B&B was perhaps our most memorable. Kevin and April were two of the happiest people in the world the following morning and called all the neighbors to share the news.

As we gathered our equipment and prepared to leave, I told Steve, "You know what they say, some days you're the prince, and some days you're the toad."

After my recent divorce and everything I had been through that summer, I was happy to have a Prince Day at the B&B.

CHAPTER 25

Devil Bear #666

"Each predator has its own tale to tell—some, like the Devil Bear, make sure they won't be forgotten."

In May 2016, a yearling heifer was killed by a grizzly. The call came in late afternoon, and it was a forty-mile drive. Knowing I'd have little time to set snares, I hooked up the culvert trap and headed in that direction.

I rarely set culvert traps. Many bears that repeatedly killed livestock had been captured or relocated in one after being caught in a snare. A few bears were foolish enough to be caught more than once, but most learned their lesson. I didn't have much faith in culverts because some bears would turn and leave upon seeing the shiny trap with the tempting bait hanging from the trigger. Stan from the Reservation once jokingly told me that he was going to have a bunch of fake culvert traps made to put around the ranches to scare off the bears.

When I arrived at the creek bottom with pine trees dotting the hillsides, it was late. The heifer was no doubt a grizzly kill—blood on the ground and bites on the back and shoulders confirmed it. There was just enough daylight to cut a hind leg off, hang it on the trigger in the culvert, and winch the remainder of the yearling into the pickup. That evening, I asked the rancher if he could drive by, check it in the morning, and let me know if the door was down.

Two days later, he called to inform us that we had a bear. I met Dave at the site. The tranquilizer was administered using a jab stick through the bars, and we slid the bear from the culvert.

It was a four-year-old, four-hundred-pound male in excellent condition—and one that had never been caught before. I felt confident he was the bear responsible, but Dave argued that many other bears were in the area, and we couldn't be sure.

We installed a collar, took measurements, and tattooed him. Every bear we worked with was assigned a number, and the next tag in the box was 666. I told Dave maybe we should toss that one and install the next. He laughed at my superstition, but time would prove me right when this "devil bear" lived up to his name.

After relocation, it didn't take long for the bear to return. The thick neck of the large boar made it difficult for the collar to stay in place, and a short time later, it fell off. The calf killing started shortly thereafter.

Weak calves from a herd battling pneumonia were easy prey. Multiple bear kills were found among them in the thick willows one morning when the ranchers came to doctor the calves.

We installed trail cameras.

Nine grizzly bears were present that night.

Devil Bear at the kill site. Notice the ear tags

Too many other healthy calves were killed that summer as well. Cameras were placed since the kills were not discovered for a couple of days. At all those different locations, one thing remained consistent. At every kill site, I obtained pictures of a large boar bear with two orange ear tags—666.

I knew he was responsible, but I needed a fresh kill to capture him. In October, my wish was granted. Another registered calf was killed. I set up cameras and cut the freshly killed calf in half, dragging it down a well-used trail on the other side of the fence. Hidden on the trail, I set two Select-A-Catch foot snares with calf parts above and below.

Early the next morning the devil bear was waiting for me when I arrived. He was in good shape and had gained one hundred seventy-five pounds over the summer.

From the time I captured him in May until October, over $35,000 was paid to producers for the calves that bear had killed. Even though bear numbers increased yearly, it would be several years before another calf kill would be found in the area, proving that 666 had been the bear responsible for all that destruction.

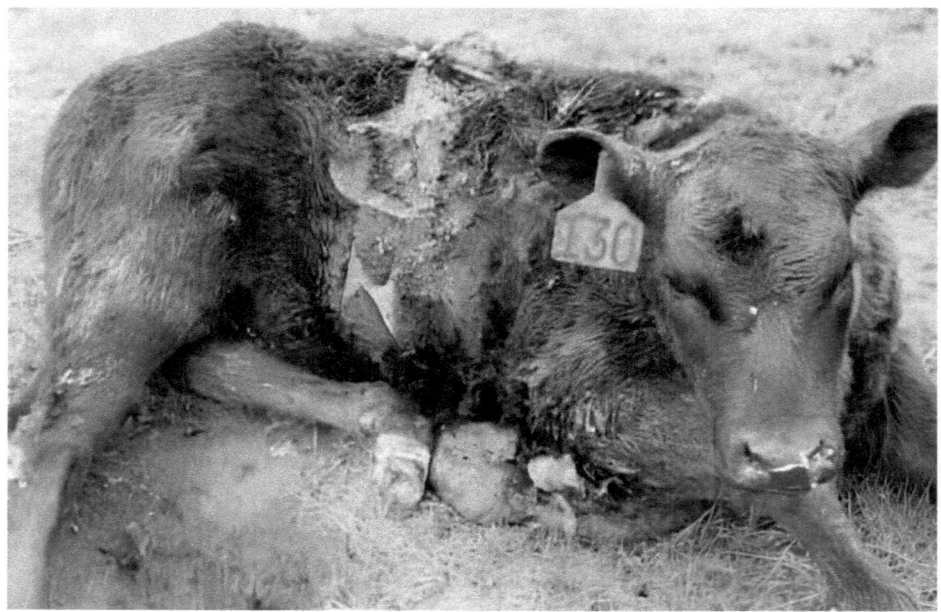

A young calf, victim of a grizzly attack, minutes before being euthanized

CHAPTER 26

Tagged for Trouble

*"Caught between predators, politics,
and the unpredictable wild."*

Throughout my career, I was often stuck in the middle. Working with other agencies, ranchers, and the public was a challenge. Every year, my wildlife job changed, yet, in many ways, it remained the same.

By 2017, the days of flying in the helicopter two or three times per month were over; sheep numbers had fallen, and coyote work had decreased. However, the increase in wolves and grizzlies more than made up for this. Work at times was hectic, especially from March through October.

But that's how I liked it.

Utilizing cattle petition money (fifty cents to a dollar per cow) and a tribal flying agreement (paid for by ranchers requesting service), I flew in the helicopter about fifty hours a year. Calving started for some in January, but most waited until March and April for warmer weather and longer days.

January through April was an ideal time to fly to decrease coyote numbers on the calving ranges and eliminate mating pairs in sheep country that would have pups by May. On the sheep range, removing these pairs helped throughout the summer since most sheep predation stemmed from family groups. Coyotes tended to travel little that time of year, so flying during that period also decreased the likelihood of other coyotes taking their place. Removing these pairs saved countless lambs.

In the spring of 2017, I was dealing with a hungry pack of wolves. They had killed several calves, including four in one night on a ranch in Teton County. One of the wolves wore a GPS collar transmitting a satellite signal twice daily to track its location. The collar confirmed that its pack was responsible for the Teton County depredations and several others to the north. The pack's home range was approximately fifty miles long and ten miles wide, totaling five hundred square miles.

The male wolf had been trapped the summer before and fitted with a GPS collar by the state wolf biologist. I later discovered, however, that the VHF signal I needed to locate the wolf from the helicopter was inoperable. The biologist had apparently known the collar was not working and had chosen to use it anyway, not bothering to switch it out for a VHF collar without GPS. While the GPS aided us in obtaining wolf locations by satellite twice a day, the VHF was necessary during a control action because it pinpointed the location of the wolf and the rest of the pack.

The wolves continued their calf killing, and my only chance to stop this was the helicopter.

I searched for wolves three times, utilizing their last GPS locations. It was a costly endeavor with little chance of success. To make matters worse, the producers partly paid for the flights and weren't pleased with our lack of results. Many people were watching us, and I knew a VHF collar on another pack member would be our only way to stop the predation.

Trying to capture a wolf in a five-hundred-square-mile area was a challenge. On top of that, we faced poor weather—snow and freezing conditions. The hunting season had started early and was to continue until the first part of January on the Reservation. With that in mind, we also risked losing our equipment or animals with all the traffic.

Then there were the bears, elk, moose, cattle, and horses that made trapping difficult. Fortunately, we had Select-A-Catch foot snares for wolves. The eleven-inch loop device came equipped with a tension bolt on the pan to avoid capturing most smaller non-target animals. Also, it had a breakaway device that opened the snare to release most larger non-targets. Upon capture, the chain wrapped around the wolf's foot, which helped maintain circulation and promoted a speedier recovery. I slept better at night because of this.

The GPS collar was helpful as it gave us an idea of where the wolves lived. Because the FWP biologist shared those locations with me, we knew they spent most of their time in a basin on the south end of the Reservation.

One morning, I drove forty-five miles to the location indicated by the GPS. There, I found wolf tracks and several likely-looking places along trails, so I set eight foot snares.

The basin was located at the foot of the Rockies. The lower end was covered with thick aspens that extended westward toward the pine country at the base of the mountain range. A creek ran through the bottom; deer, elk, and bears lived there. It was cattle country in the summer, with many horses, some wild and some not. Our trapping efforts would be easier before the cattle arrived, so time was limited.

After checking empty sets for two days, I met with Andy, a tribal game warden. He was a thirty-year-old, six-foot-four, two-hundred seventy-five-pound Native with thick black hair that fell to his shoulder blades. He was a gentle giant of a man in the prime of his life. Fortunately, his good nature was as broad as his shoulders, and as I would find out later, he was fearless. Andy and I planned to work together to capture and collar a wolf.

Scouting the basin, we found where the wolves had passed through the day before. We placed another nine sets on trails, hoping the wolves would return. The more sets we had out, the better our chances.

Andy was a natural and dedicated trapper, having worked with Stan (the tribal biologist) trapping grizzly bears before becoming a warden. He already knew bears and was a most willing student. His positive attitude brightened any situation; he was always fun to be around.

Checking our foot snares the following day, we discovered the first set had captured a horse. The snare was anchored solidly, and judging by the tracks, the snare had done as designed, opening with the power of the horse's first pull and immediately releasing him. That was the only action that day, as the rest of the sets remained empty.

Two days later, while hunting coyotes in the helicopter, I noticed three missed calls from Andy on my cell phone. Upon landing and checking messages, Andy's voicemail reported, "We captured a one-hundred-pound black bear, and it's still there."

Several times in the past, we had caught big grizzlies, and like the horse, they had opened the breakaway and escaped. Unfortunately, the snare could hold smaller bears since they were closer in weight to wolves. I called Andy and told him we were on our way.

The Hughes 500 helicopter cruised at one-hundred-twenty miles per hour, and in no time, we arrived. We met Andy a mile east of the trap site. He had estimated the bear's weight and said it was in good shape. We then loaded a dart with just enough sedative to enable us to remove the snare from its wrist. Andy and I drove to the trap site in his pickup, and the darting went off without a hitch. The bear, unharmed, was soon released.

The equipment was checked every morning by 8 a.m. A day after the black bear was caught, I made my usual rounds but found nothing. I remembered an opening in the trees that contained a cow salt lick a half mile west of the last set, so I headed in that direction, thinking it would be an excellent place for another snare.

When I emerged from the thick trees into a clearing, I found two sub-adult grizzlies staring at me twenty yards away, exactly where I was about to place the snare. I turned around, glad to be in the safety of the pickup. Even with the selective foot snares, trapping around bears was nerve-racking.

Two days later, early in the morning, Andy and I were halfway through the line when we came around a corner to find a pale-colored animal in one of Andy's trail sets.

It was a wolf.

And not just any wolf, but the alpha male that wore the non-functioning collar!

Andy had caught his first wolf, and what a wolf it was!

We were relieved to see him there but worried he might escape if not well caught. It had snowed lightly the night before, and we could see no evidence of other wolves. However, circling the trap site were tracks of a medium-sized grizzly, putting us on guard.

I don't remember being so nervous or excited. Everyone had been watching our operation: the ranchers losing the calves, FWP, my agency, Wildlife Services, and the Tribe. Thousands of dollars of calves had already been killed, and a lot of money had been spent toward our efforts.

We slowly walked toward the big wolf with a shotgun to see how well he was caught and to be sure the cable was not frayed. Upon examination, we discovered everything looked great, an excellent catch. The wolf wasn't struggling against the snare in any way. Instead, he stared at us and started barking like a dog. The barking continued periodically for the fifteen minutes it took us to load the dart and tranquilize him, which gave me an eerie feeling. Once the dart was in place, we relaxed.

Wolf captured in a Select-A-Catch

Andy and I were happier than words could express when we finally replaced the collar around his neck. We were even more elated to remove our equipment and finally be finished with our daily trap checks.

The data from the GPS collar, transmitting two daily locations, showed the wolf moved three miles north the day it was captured—an impressive distance. The recovery had been rapid compared to our previous methods, which sometimes took several days to recover from. The longer it took a wolf to heal, the longer it took for the collar to lead us back to its pack.

I had a helicopter flight scheduled four days after the wolf was captured. That morning, we went north using the VHF signal to search for the wolf. From the capture site, we continued flying north. After proceeding ten miles, we were unable to identify the signal. I texted the FWP wolf specialist and asked him to provide the last GPS location he had received that morning, hoping that would help. He informed us that the signal had come from even farther north, past where we had turned around. A high ridge had blocked the way, and since the VHF transmission was line-of-site, we hadn't been able to receive it. We headed north again, and soon after passing over the ridge, we heard the collar.

Flying along the creek bottom, we heard the signal grow louder. We observed two grizzlies feeding on a dead cow. The pines and aspens were widespread but not dense. If the wolves were there, we should be able to see them. With the high number of calves previously killed by this pack, we planned to remove at least part of them. The collared wolf would be the last to go.

Suddenly, a wolf appeared, trotting up the creek bottom below us. It was our collar, walking without a limp like nothing had happened. If the others were there, they would be close by. We thoroughly searched the area but determined he was alone. We'd have to try again some other time and hope to find the pack together.

I was impressed not only with Andy but with the foot snare. The wolf we located that day was unharmed and had traveled twelve miles from the capture site. Over the next two years, the radio collar helped us locate and remove several wolves from the pack when calves were killed. Our collared wolf eventually met its end when it was shot by a deer hunter with a wolf tag thirty miles south of where he had been captured.

Andy went to work for our agency shortly after we collared the wolf. During the last part of my career, he and I had many more exciting wolf and bear experiences.

Now that I have retired, what I miss most is the country, people, and adventures working on the Blackfeet Reservation. It was a special time of my life that will never be forgotten.

UNEXPLAINED MUTILATIONS

CHAPTER 27

Unexplained Mutilations

*"Some say it's predators; some call it a hoax.
I call it unexplainable."*

Over the years, I was asked, more times than I would like, what my thoughts were on cattle mutilations. People in this small part of Montana knew that because of my job, I had investigated more livestock deaths than most, and a small part of those investigations involved mutilations. All I could ever say was that I didn't know what had caused them, but that they definitely weren't the work of predators or cults.

One Saturday afternoon in late September 2016, a rancher who lived west along the mountainfront called to inform me that he had found another "damn mutilation," a large Charolais bull. Since the 1970s, the area had been a hotspot for mutilation reports, so I wasn't surprised to get the call.

Three weeks before, wolves had killed a cow not far from where the bull was discovered. Investigating mutilations was not part of my job, and even though the rancher thought the bull was mutilated, I worried wolves could be involved and agreed to take a look.

It was an hour from my house to the ranch. When I arrived, I found the deputy from Conrad, the neighboring ranchers who owned the two-year-old bull, and the local game warden waiting. The ranch was private property with limited access; most gates remained locked at that time of year. The bull lay three miles from the county road down an old dirt trail. It was in a depression near a small pond and could not be easily seen from any direction. During the summer, cattle required little attention, so the rancher was fortunate to have found the massive white bull when he had.

Starting the examination, I first noticed that the left side

Head of the Charolais bull, showing precision cuts and a missing tongue

of the bull's head was neatly skinned. The incision started from the ear and led down to the nose. From there, the hide had been removed below the lower part of the eye to the back and bottom of the jaw. The cut was precise and exposed the opening on the bottom, revealing that the tongue had been removed at the top of the throat with one straight slice. On the ground beneath the bull was a large, dried pool of blood that told me the animal might not have been dead when this occurred. We also found another pool of blood, the size of a basketball, where it had bled out the rectum.

This was different from any mutilation I had previously seen. Animals did not bleed that much after they were dead, and it was strange that it had also bled from the rectum.

The left legs stuck up and outward, and what I saw next surprised me. The

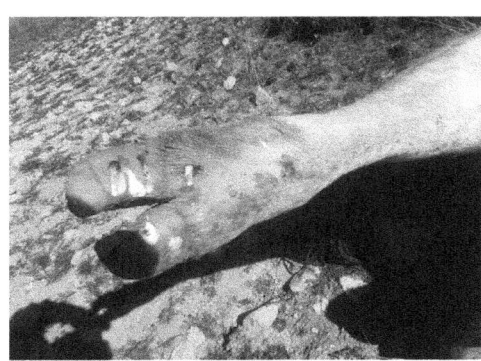

The bloody red markings (white is bird droppings) found on the bull's leg

lower part of both legs showed blood-smeared markings. Three two-inch lines were found above the hoof on one leg as if bloody fingers had left their mark. It looked like a bloody hand had tried moving the bull from side to side by pulling its leg. Other than on the legs and around the rectum, there was no blood on the outside of the snow-white bull.

We began the necropsy by skinning the upper side; there, we found extensive hemorrhaging along the front end, side, and into the hindquarters indicative of injuries that had occurred while the animal was still alive. It was as if it had been hit by a train, except we were a long way from railroad tracks or a good road for that matter. Being located on the upper side only reinforced my thought that the bull had been moved.

"Could it have been dropped?" the warden asked.

Next, we examined the intestines. They were whitish-yellow, including the heart and lungs. One lung even showed signs of deterioration. When we finished, we still had no answers. Given the circumstances, I was glad the ranchers were there, as they were just as confused as we were.

We spread out to search the area but found no tracks from predators or vehicles. If predators had been involved, we would have seen tracks around the pond.

The next test was to see if anything would feed on the carcass in the coming days. Often, predators refused to eat freshly mutilated animals. If they did, it was only after a few days had passed. The previous month, wolves had killed a lame, full-grown cow a short distance from there. That cow had been devoured in three days.

Two days later, the rancher called again. "You're not going to believe this, but I found *another* mutilated cow, about two miles from the bull."

"Is it fresh?" I asked.

"No, I think it happened around the same time as the bull. It's a yearling heifer." The rancher paused. "The side of the head and bottom jaw have been skinned, and the tongue's been cut straight at the throat, like the bull. I spotted a grizzly near the carcass, but the cow's not been fed on. I checked the bull too. It's not been touched either. Not even by the birds."

I couldn't wait to see this last one and asked if he could email me a photo.

After examining the picture, it was clear that this wasn't the work of animals. The hide on the side of the head was skinned, similar to the bull, from the eye down to the lower jaw. One difference was the hide above the eye was skinned clean about an inch out from the socket in a half-circle shape. The photo revealed a dark void where the eye should have been, and the rancher reported that when he looked inside, it seemed hollow.

Days later, a veterinarian friend examined the picture and jokingly said, "It looks as if the hide was removed to get a good vacuum around the eye socket to suck everything out."

The yearling heifer skinned with its eyes and tongue missing

Two weeks later, bears started eating both carcasses. Whatever was stopping them before must have gone away.

While all this mutilation business was taking place, I had traps set on the north end of the Reservation, hoping to capture and collar a wolf. The trapline was far from home and needed to be checked daily. Luckily, the tribal wardens could inspect them the mornings I was unavailable.

A few days after the mutilations, I was checking my wolf foot snare line with an older warden. He informed me that a couple of days earlier, Donny, a young tribal warden, had been scared shitless while driving on the south end of the Reservation. Donny had told him something about a bright light coming over the pickup, but the warden didn't know the details.

Later that day, I called Donny. I knew him well; we had worked together when he was a tribal bear manager before becoming a warden. He was honest and a great guy.

"I had been working late in a remote area with another warden on the south end of the Reservation. We came out of the trees to a gate. When I got out to open the gate, I saw a massive light in the sky heading toward us from the south," explained Donny.

"How big was the light?" I asked.

"The size of a car."

"About how high up was it?"

"The height of a telephone pole," Donny replied. "The strangest part was there was no sound. It just silently passed over us and headed north."

A Bureau of Indian Affairs officer had also witnessed the light a few minutes later as it had moved northward.

"When did this happen?" I asked Donny.

"Last week."

"What day?"

"Friday."

That was the same night the mutilations had occurred. It wasn't that far away.

Almost every working day, I investigated dead livestock. Sometimes they were killed, and other times, they just died and were fed on by predators. I had primarily dealt with sheep and coyote predation during the first ten years of my career and had never seen anything strange.

For the next thirty years, I was involved with cattle depredations involving grizzlies and wolves. In a five-county area, I was the official responsible for determining the cause of death for reimbursement on depredations caused by these two large predators.

My first mutilation experience occurred in 1992. From then on, they continued until I retired in 2020.

Investigating a depredation was like investigating a crime scene. First, we searched for predator signs such as tracks and scat. Then I moved on to the necropsy of the livestock. Sometimes, the animal was totally consumed, which made it difficult to determine its cause of death. If multiple predators, like bears, wolves, lions, or coyotes, were in the area, it became a real challenge to pinpoint the culprit. Sometimes, livestock was killed by one predator and fed upon by another. Other times, livestock just died and were simply fed on. I was the only official in my district that could verify a kill for compensation.

After taking pictures, I examined the outside for bite marks and scratches, then started skinning. Often, what I saw on the outside differed from what I found on the inside. For example, I might have seen scratches and teeth marks on the hide, but when I skinned it back, I found the flesh light-colored with no bloody hemorrhage underneath. That told me the bites or scratches had occurred after the animal died. On the other hand, blood and hemorrhaging under the hide were indicative of trauma that had occurred while the animal was alive. That usually confirmed predation as the cause of death.

Sometimes, the carcasses were consumed so that only the hide remained. That happened often with bears as they could skin a cow better than a butcher. Taking the dirty hide to water and washing it would usually show dark-red hemorrhaging around the teeth marks if it had been killed. Even though it was too late to catch the bear or wolf responsible, the rancher would still receive compensation.

Each animal had its own unique way of killing.

Bears tended to bite on the top of the shoulder, back, and atop the nose.

Coyotes usually went for the bottom of the throat.

Lions targeted the top and sides of the neck and consumed the front shoulder.

Wolves bit behind the front legs, along the back of the rear legs, and under or on the side of the throat.

These methods were typical but could vary.

At the publication of this book, payment to a rancher in Montana is made on all verified and probable grizzly, wolf, and lion depredations. No reimbursement is paid for injured livestock unless they die later from their injuries. USDA Wildlife Services in Montana has the final say on whether the animal is killed or not for reimbursement.

In 1992, when I first started examining cattle mutilations, I found that they were unlike anything I had ever seen. Before then, like many other people, I had laughed them off.

Over the next fifteen years, however, I experienced a random summer with a rash of mutilations; then, I went two or three years without any. However, the last fifteen years of my career found me investigating these strange occurrences *every* summer. There were also cases I heard of but never examined. In this remote part of Montana, many were never even found.

I didn't take pictures in the early years because I knew how controversial the topic was. I didn't want to deal with interview requests or being called in to testify. The last thing I wanted was for people to think I was crazy, so I kept quiet.

A typical mutilation consisted of one side of the head being skinned and the tongue being cut off, removed at the top of the throat. Sometimes, the whole side of the head was skinned, while at other times, it was peeled from the eye down. The head was often skinned downwards to the bottom of the lower jaw, making it easier to extract the tongue.

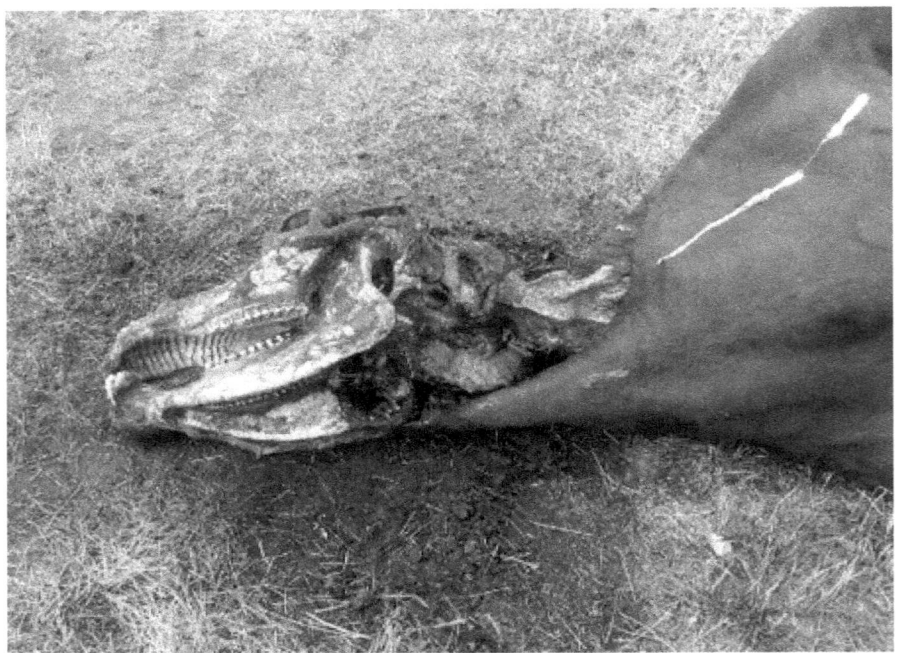
Strange method of removing the flesh, leaving the bone white

Strangely, on some, the flesh was entirely cleaned from the bone, leaving behind a pale white color with no sign of knife or teeth marks. It was almost as if a laser had completed the brutal task. In most cases, the eye was missing, like it had been cleanly removed rather than pecked out by birds. Quite a few but not all had the udder and genitals missing.

Most of my investigations took place on private property with limited public access; some were behind locked gates. While my job didn't typically involve investigating such incidents, I often went as I not only wanted to rule out predators but to learn more about the strange occurrences.

One of my strangest cases happened in 2000 and involved an older rancher. He said he had hesitated to call, but that there was something he wanted me to look at. I had known him for years. He was a wiry old man, soft-spoken, and well thought of.

When I arrived, we drove a mile west of his house on private land to the yearling cow pasture. As we reached the top of the hill, I noticed the skeleton of an Angus yearling below us. From a distance, I could see something strange about it. The nine-hundred-pound yearling had been totally consumed, yet there wasn't a tromped-down outer circle in the tall grass surrounding it. Predators always matted the grass down as they devoured a carcass. As we drew closer, I realized that the skeleton was clean, with no sinew or hide remaining. It almost looked like the bones had been boiled.

The grass stood ten inches high, and it looked like the skeleton had been placed there. The only hide that remained was a thin strip on top of each hoof, cut in a straight line. I lifted the skull from the ground. The tongue was missing, and the head felt unusually light and hollow.

The rumen, the contents of the stomach, lay a few feet away in the tall grass. I studied the scene for a long moment in silence before turning to search for predator signs. After thirty minutes, I found nothing.

Later, as we stood beside the remains, I asked the rancher, "When did you discover this?"

"Three days ago," he replied. "I had driven past here the evening before and saw nothing. But early that next morning, it was there."

"Do the remains look different to you now compared to when you first found it?"

He shook his head. "No. They're exactly the same, except when I first discovered it, the bones were red and shiny."

Another memorable case happened in 2019.

That year was busy, and I examined more mutilations than I cared to. I got a call from a rancher claiming their biggest calf had been cut in half, and its hindquarters were missing. At first, I thought it might just be someone helping themselves to some beef along the county road. After learning the location was on private property three miles from the main road with no public access. I realized there might be more to the story.

"The weird thing is," she added, "there was no blood on the ground."

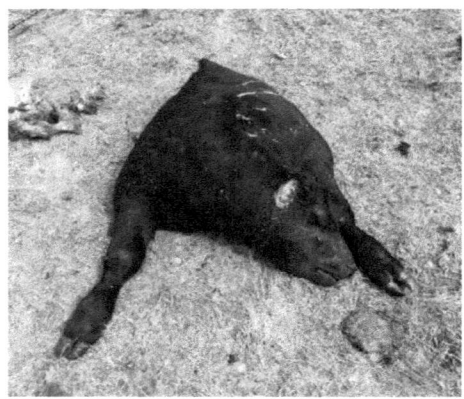
The calf cut in half. Its ear bears the football-shaped cutout described.

The next morning, I met the ranchers at their house before we traveled the rough two-track trail to the site.

The four-hundred-fifty-pound calf was in an unusual position, on its sternum with both front legs spread out on each side of its head. The head was cocked to one side, and the calf had been cleanly cut in two, with its loin and hindquarters removed. The left ear was missing, sliced off in a football-shaped cut, so no ear tag was found for identification.

Furthermore, the section of hide that would have shown the brand was gone as well. Nearby several small bones lay together, clean with no teeth marks. The ranchers had searched the area extensively with four-wheelers the day before, but the large leg bones and pelvis hadn't been found. The calf was hidden in a low spot and could not be seen at a distance from any direction. The only tire tracks were those from the ranchers.

When the calf was discovered the previous evening, they had covered the carcass with a tarp to prevent animals from scavenging on it. Driving in that morning, they told me it was their biggest and best calf, not realizing they even had calves that big.

I began my necropsy, finding no sign of blood or bite marks. I had brought my metal detector and searched the calf's remains for bullets—nothing. I next looked for scat or tracks from predators but came up with the same results. Finding no blood had me wondering. A depredation or simply cutting a calf in half should have left blood.

After putting on rubber gloves, I reached into the chest cavity and removed the intact heart and lungs. Surprisingly, they were dry, and there was no sign of blood pooling at the bottom of the chest cavity. Using my knife, I then made an incision on the top of the backbone and skinned down both sides of the front shoulders, searching for any kind of trauma. The meat appeared anemic and pale. The head was intact except for the cut-off ear.

Lastly, I pried open the tightly closed mouth to discover the tongue missing, cut straight off three-quarters of the way in.

That was *enough*!

The absence of blood on the ground, the calf lying on its sternum, the cut-off tongue, and the way the ear was removed all told me that a predator hadn't done this. After what they had just seen, the ranchers seemed to agree.

Later that fall, I received *another* call from the same people. They explained that they had shipped their calves and to their surprise, none had been missing. Therefore, the mutilated calf from earlier in the summer couldn't have been theirs. It must have belonged to someone else, which would explain why it had been so much bigger than the others.

They then asked, "Could it have been dropped from somewhere else?"

With no missing calf, no ear tag or blood on the ground, I replied, "Maybe..."

Their area of Montana was desolate with ranches few and far between. Three weeks later, ten miles to the west, another rancher called to report a dead calf. He told me he thought there must be a lot of coyotes for much had been eaten; he worried about his sheep. I didn't say it then but thought it was a bear. That same ranch had experienced a visit from a grizzly two years prior; though unlikely, it wasn't out of the question.

The rancher described the location: two miles from the county road through two tight gates. The cattle had been moved into the pasture for only three days and were being removed that morning when the calf had been discovered. The first gate entering the pasture was so tight that I needed a Goldenrod fence stretcher to open it. With my pickup, I followed the rancher's four-wheeler tracks in the tall grass for about a half mile until I spotted the calf in the middle of the pasture. The terrain was rolling hills, and as usual, it was in a low spot. There were no other tire tracks except those made by the rancher.

The three-hundred-fifty-pound calf was lying on its left side. Its body had been sliced straight from the lower front part of its hindquarters, diagonally across the ribs to the upper shoulder, and down to the sternum behind the front leg. All the intestines had been removed.

I noticed two short pieces (six inches long) of intestine lying beside it on the ground. Then, totally out of place, I saw the calf's liver lying in the grass ten feet away, intact, showing no sign of teeth marks. Usually, that was the first thing a predator ate, and the lack of teeth marks made me wonder how it got there. I also noticed the right ear was missing, cut off in an oddly familiar shape. It appeared similar to the calf I had investigated a couple of weeks before.

The rancher had told me he had the calf's ear tag, so I called him on my cell phone. "Did you cut the ear off to retrieve the tag?"

"No," he replied. "The tag was lying on the ground, and I didn't see the ear."

That was strange as the ear tag was attached with a plastic button through the opposite side of the ear, connected, and locked so it remained firmly in place. Usually, the button was cut off from the back to remove a tag.

"Was the button still attached?" I asked.

"Yes!"

"Were there any teeth marks on the tag?"

The rancher thought and then slowly replied, "No."

"So, how could an animal remove the ear tag from a thick calf ear with the button *still* attached?"

"I have no idea." He replied

I knew from the evidence that predators were not involved. I grabbed two trail cameras from my pickup and set them around the carcass thirty feet apart, hoping to solve the mystery.

A week passed before I returned for my cameras, eager to see what I'd find. The calf remained untouched except for being pecked on by birds. I retrieved the cameras and headed home, where I would examine the photos on the computer.

One coyote picture was taken that week, but it had only passed by, not bothering to feed. Weirdly enough, for a month following this necropsy, the upper part of my legs hurt. That, coupled with the fact that my watch had stopped while examining a mutilated cow the year before, started me thinking that it would be smart to avoid handling the carcasses. That was the last necropsy I ever performed on a mutilation.

While most mutilations were cattle, I also investigated cases involving sheep, horses, and bison. Some claimed predators, cults, or black helicopters were the cause. I didn't agree. After years of examining mutilated livestock, I wondered if there wasn't something else here. I've been asked many times for interviews but have declined each one.

If you decide to search "cattle mutilation images" on the computer, be prepared to see similar photos from Europe, South America, and other countries. They're all strange, to say the least.

CHAPTER 28

Jade and the Bears of Dupuyer Creek

"Loyalty, courage, and a bond stronger than fear."

Public signage warning of the presence of a foot snare

Most people never get the chance to take their dog to work, but I did.

As I reached the later stages of my career, my old Border Collie, Brindie, began showing her age at fourteen. She was faithful and loved going to work with me. Brindie was great at finding coyotes, and I felt more secure when she accompanied me while doing bear work. The only issue Brindie had was that she had been deaf since she was a pup. So, we created our own form of sign language to communicate. I thought about getting another work dog but wondered if that would be necessary so close to retirement.

In March, while preparing to fly in the helicopter, one of my co-workers, Randy, arrived to pull the fuel trailer to the north country, where we planned to hunt coyotes. While having a cup of coffee at my house, he told us he had a male German Wachtelhund and had recently purchased a female of the same breed from a co-worker. Randy had gotten a great deal on her, but under the condition that she would be spayed.

The Wachtelhund originated from Germany and was known for being a great hunting dog with a gentle personality. Randy admitted he didn't get the female spayed, and that morning, she had given birth to six pups. He didn't know what to do and was sure our co-worker wouldn't be happy. I glanced at my wife, Maureen, knowing this would be a commitment for both of us, likely for many years. She smiled and understood my thoughts. When I offered to buy one of the pups, he said that, under the circumstances, he couldn't charge us, and that's how Jade came into our lives eight weeks later.

With her beautiful auburn coat, she looked like a cross between a Cocker Spaniel and a Brittany. Her unique amber eyes were almost human-like.

Jade

Going through the puppy phase, she chewed on everything—garden hoses and shoes—and forced us to spend more money than anticipated on our *free* dog. We chuckled between ourselves, "Why did we decide to do this again?" With the amount it took to get her spayed and the $800 operation for a broken leg she had incurred at six months old, she was proving to be as expensive as raising a kid! Despite all of that, what devotion she showed toward Maureen and myself. She became part of our family and has been worth every penny.

In June 2019, I received a call about a calf depredation caused by a grizzly in lower Dupuyer Creek, close to the town of Valier. I headed in that direction, accompanied by Jade. She loved nothing more than to go to work every day and was a big help.

I met with the MFWP bear specialist Les and his assistant Carol at the scene. The kill site was thirty miles from the mountains, along a brushy creek bottom lined with spans of cottonwood trees.

There were clear signs of a grizzly attack: bite marks on the shoulders and a pool of blood on the ground next to the half-eaten calf. The ground was hard, so we couldn't find any measurable tracks.

I spotted a grove of cottonwood trees on the east side of the creek, four hundred yards away—an excellent spot to drag the carcass and set foot snares. I asked Les to set up a culvert trap using part of the calf for bait at the kill site.

I drove to the edge of the trees and removed two pipe sets from my pickup. They were my snare setup of choice when dealing with livestock depredations as cattle were usually still in the pasture. By design, they couldn't get caught in the traps.

Now, I hate to admit this, but at that point in my career, I had grown complacent, not bothering to carry my shotgun or pepper spray with me that beautiful, calm morning. I had thought it was a low-risk situation and speculated that the bear was likely west on the creek bottom, sleeping in its day bed.

The small grove of cottonwoods sat at the base of a brush-covered hillside northeast of the creek and was sixty yards from the thick tree line to the west.

Forty yards from my pickup, I finished the first pipe set, placing a rock on top to prevent capturing a cow. I was on my knees, intently working on the second set, when Jade, who never barked unless there was a reason, let out an alarming growl followed by a loud bark and took off running to the southwest.

I sat up in time to see a yearling grizzly cub running alongside me up the hill to my left, fifteen yards away. I was still on my knees, unprotected and in a bad position. When I jumped to my feet, I saw the sow grizzly fifty yards away running in the opposite direction, with Jade chasing her across the creek toward the trees from where she had come.

And there I was—in the middle!

After all these years, how could I have let this happen?

I yelled at Jade to return, hoping the bear would not follow. My heart raced as I ran toward the pickup for my shotgun. Sows with cubs were considered extremely dangerous, defending their cubs or protecting a kill site. In this case, it was both.

I spotted Les and Carol roaring toward me in their pickup. They had heard Jade and seen the bear. Jade hurried back to me and I gave her the biggest hug. I had been so intent on setting the snare that I had placed myself between the sow and cub. Had it not been for Jade...

After things calmed down, I finished setting the snares. The culvert trap was placed at the kill site and two snares were set in the trees should the bears return. The following morning would be an interesting one.

I left the next day before sunrise. Even after forty years, I was still tense with anticipation and excitement. My job of protecting livestock from predators never lost its meaning.

Les lived a short distance away, and driving into the trap site that morning, I saw he was already there. I shifted my gaze to the snares, expecting to see a bear, but they were empty. Les and Carol stood beside the culvert trap. They had captured a sub-adult grizzly.

While examining my sets that morning, I discovered that both snares had been sprung.

I anxiously studied the photos from the trail cameras and found at least four other grizzlies had visited the site the night before, not including the young male captured in the culvert trap. The same sow that had approached me while setting the snares and her cub were included in the pictures. The photos revealed how the cub, as they often did, was the one who had dug at and sprung the snares. Of all the bears, it was the sow we needed to capture.

At that time, another vehicle joined us. Kevin, a rancher who neighbored to the south, informed us he had found a calf killed the night before in his herd. Les and I jumped in my pickup and followed Kevin to the kill site a mile away.

There was no doubt that the calf had been killed by a grizzly; one-third of it had been consumed. Hoping the bear would follow the trail, we dragged the calf two hundred yards to the other side of the pasture fence so the cows wouldn't wreck my set. The rancher and MFWP helped construct a pen while I set the snare.

Because we didn't have any trees to use, we created the trap using a wooden snow fence that was just wide enough for a bear to enter. We positioned the carcass—our bait—inside toward the back of the enclosed circle, and I set a foot snare in the entrance. We attached a four-hundred-pound weight to the chain and placed a camera aimed at the trap site.

We then returned to the original location, tranquilized, and processed the bear in the culvert. It was a young male weighing two hundred seventy-five pounds. After taking data and tagging and collaring him, we transferred the bear into a double culvert owned by MFWP and gave him water.

The family trap, or double culvert trap, was a long barrel that kept a locked bear on one side while the opposite end remained open. A wall of bars split the two compartments. If a second bear entered through the still-open end, it would step on a treadle in the floor causing the door to close behind it. This was commonly used for sows and their cubs. So, we reset the pipe sets and added two more.

That night, the bears returned.

Les, Carol, and the rancher were there when I arrived the next day. Topping the hill, I spied two bears caught in foot snares. They were calm and quiet but became agitated and vocal as I drove closer. The yearling was unsurprisingly the loudest. We spotted the sow twice across the creek two hundred yards away. She watched us a moment, then disappeared into the trees.

They were young bears; the two-year-old was already tagged, having been captured as a nuisance bear the year before. The other was the yearling cub that had dug up our snares the previous night. The culvert was empty; one of the pipe sets had been dug, but the last snare remained armed. That told me the old sow we were dealing with was intelligent, as she hadn't fallen for the pipe or culvert sets despite spending a lot of time with the captured bears.

While Les mixed the tranquilizer, I left to check the pen set a mile away. Accompanying me was our trapper from the south, Kirk, who had joined us that morning. As it turned out, we were going to need his help.

Just as we were leaving to check the snare at the second site, Kevin drove in, looking more unhappy than the day before. He informed us that a bear had killed one of his cows during the night, close to where he had lost the calf the previous day.

Kirk and I arrived at the kill site, only a quarter mile from the snow fence pen set. The trap could not be seen as it was over a hill. Considering the latest carnage, we hoped the bear responsible would be waiting for us there.

It was an older cow, bitten on the nostrum and on top of the shoulders in typical grizzly fashion. However, something was different about this kill; it had not been fed upon, simply killed and abandoned with its head left lying in a pool of blood.

After examining the cow, we headed to the nearby snare site. When we topped the hill, we saw the pen demolished and found a two-hundred-fifty-pound young grizzly waiting for us. It was disappointing as I knew this bear hadn't killed the cow. The real culprit would have been larger and more powerful. A smaller bear would not have made such a clean kill and would have eaten something afterward.

I had also noticed when skinning the cow earlier that there had been a lack of canine punctures through the hide where it had been bitten. That happened when an animal was killed by an old bear with canine teeth worn by age, not a younger bear like the one we had caught. I figured the cow had been killed by the old sow we had pictures of at the first site. I had earlier suspected she was also responsible for the calf kill. More than likely, the mother bear had taken out her frustrations on the cow after her cub was captured.

We returned to the first location to help with the two captured bears. MFWP did most of the processing, and we assisted however we could. The first bear with blue ear tags had been captured by MFWP the previous summer. It hung around the town of Valier and Lake Francis and seemed to have little fear of people. When she was caught, the young female was relocated to the west, only to return a short time later. However, after the trapping experience, she seemed to have more respect for humans.

The second bear was a yearling male that had dug up our snares the night before. This time, he had made a mistake and been caught! It was a gangly bear of one hundred forty pounds. As all yearling grizzlies do when captured, he was very vocal, letting us know he wasn't happy. Not knowing the whereabouts of the sow, I kept the shotgun close by.

The blue-tagged bear was tranquilized and fitted with a new collar. It may have been a previous offspring of the old female and was traveling with her. Since the bear had already been tagged and identified, little time was spent processing her. That one and the bear in the culvert from the night before would be relocated, as we felt confident they had not been involved in the kills.

The yearling was then processed, taking longer as it was necessary to tag, tattoo, and place a PIT tag for identification under the hide. We hurried. We still had one more bear waiting for us up the creek.

FWP drove a few miles away and released the young male captured the first night. After the yearling was processed, we placed him in the front section of the family trap where the young male had been the night before. There was a chance its mother would return after dark and enter the other side. If not, my only option to catch her would be to set different types of snares. That was possible now, as the cows had avoided this place since we started capturing bears.

When finished, we went up to the creek to our third capture. The bear was patiently waiting, and in no time, he was processed and placed in a culvert trap for relocation. That evening, he was released forty miles away, along with the blue-tagged bear.

Now to the sow... I knew capturing her would not be an easy task, and I had only one night left. If we failed, the yearling would have to be released on-site, as he was too young to be taken from his mother. I knew the old bear would stay and continue killing if that happened. The ranchers were starting to get concerned.

The U.S. Fish & Wildlife Service (USFWS) was also growing restless, but in another way. They informed us that we were capturing too many non-target bears. In fact, USFWS told Les that I was finished setting snares.

"The snares are our only chance!" I angrily told Les, more than a little put out with USFWS.

"I know," Les muttered.

"Well, if the snares can't be set, then you need to sit in a tree above the culvert trap *tonight* and dart that sow when she returns."

I knew the cub in our possession was our only chance to lure in this cow-killer. Fortunately, after explaining my concerns to them, the USFWS changed its mind and permitted me to set one more night.

We left for lunch and returned to the site that afternoon. The cow was hauled away to avoid attracting more bears than we already had. I told Les that I believed the sow would not go into the culvert. Even if she had never been caught that way, she had likely been transported in one at some point. She was a trap-wise, intelligent bear. A blind trail set was my only option.

Looking the area over, I noticed an opening between the back corner of the culvert trap and a nearby tree. This was a perfect tree to anchor to, with no low branches and just enough space for a bear to go between the tree and the culvert. I could hide a snare for when the bear returned in search of her cub.

I took a Select-A-Catch 3000 (a foot snare) with a sixteen-inch cable loop and set it in the opening on the trail. The set took no time to put in place and was carefully concealed. It was late, and I hurried to finish, knowing she would soon return. MFWP installed two trail cameras while I set the snare.

Getting a good night's sleep was always difficult, and getting out of bed at 4:30 took little effort. I got into the pickup and drove to the trap site, anxious to see what had transpired overnight. It would go one way or the other, with no in-between.

I arrived just as it was light enough to see; I was the only one there. Slowly driving down the short hill into the trap site, I was not surprised to see the culvert door open, and the pipe sets empty. Everything looked the same as the evening before. When I reached the bottom, I could finally see the other side of the long culvert trap where the trail snare was set.

And there she was, captured in my snare.

The old sow stood to intently watch me. She was a large bear for a female and looked tired. Perfectly caught, the snare cable was attached firmly around her wrist. At that moment, a heavy weight was lifted off my shoulders.

Les and Carol pulled up behind me and were just as relieved to see the bear had been captured. They prepared the tranquilizer while I stayed with the neighbors who had started to assemble. A big part of the job was trying to keep people back in such situations. We were almost always on private property, so asking them to leave was out of the question. We also didn't want anyone getting hurt, especially if something went sideways.

Les and Carol administered the tranquilizer, and the sow went to sleep. She was in excellent shape, especially for having a cub. For an older bear, her fur was pristine. I knew she had been captured before because of how she had reacted to the snares. After removing the snare, the first thing we did was look at her teeth. They were brown and worn, as I had suspected after examining the teeth marks at the cow depredation.

Next, we folded out her upper lip, and there, as if it had recently been placed, was a blue tattoo with the number 205. I recognized the number but couldn't remember the bear. From that low of a number, I knew she had been captured many years before. At that point in my life, I seldom posed for bear pictures. However, I posed with her that day because I felt this one might be special.

When I got home and went through my records, I confirmed we had caught 205 in a pipe set *twenty-two years* before when she had been two years old at a sheep depredation site. That made her twenty-four, quite old for a bear. Searching, I discovered a picture of her and me from long ago in a photo album. Comparing the photos, my wife Maureen commented, "Well, it's clear you both got older and gained a few pounds."

I replied with a laugh, "I don't know about the bear, but my extra pounds are *your* fault!"

Later, I learned that 205 had been caught one other time raiding apple trees. That hadn't counted as a strike, so she was still on a second-strike capture. She would be allowed one more chance. After what we had just experienced, I felt it wasn't right to turn the old cow-killer loose. The only good thing I could see coming out of it was that the ranchers on Dupuyer Creek would be relieved knowing she would be hauled out of there and gone (for now).

I eagerly loaded my equipment and prepared to leave that day. I was grateful that everything had turned out as well as it had and that no one had been hurt, thanks in no small part to the best dog ever, Jade.

MFWP relocated the sow and her cub to the western side of the mountains, where livestock was scarce. Yet, I couldn't help but worry. I knew if she killed again, trying to catch her would be my responsibility. After all I'd witnessed the last few days, I realized that should she come back, that task would be close to impossible.

Less than a month later, she returned to the East Front. Shortly afterward, the collar's signal mysteriously disappeared. The following two summers, until I retired, were peaceful, with no cattle depredations on Dupuyer Creek.

Mike with Bertha—twenty-two years apart

BIG MISTAKE

AT BEAR HOLLOW

CHAPTER 29

Big Mistake at Bear Hollow

"Forty-two years of work, and the wild still had one last lesson to teach me."

After forty-two years on the job, one thing never changed: I had no idea what would happen next. Little did I realize that going into the final summer of my career, I would have the scariest bear experience of my life.

I had dealt with the wolves of Birch Creek for many years. The creek was the southern boundary of the Reservation. In the past, whenever wolves killed livestock on either side, we had successfully stopped the problem. Private trappers were permitted to pursue wolves on the south side, resulting in a few being taken. However, no matter how many Birch Creek wolves were removed, they consistently reproduced or had others join them to keep the pack going. If they weren't causing problems, they were tolerated. But when they started killing livestock, that tolerance ended.

During the summer of 2018, wolves killed several calves, and that fall, many more went missing. That was financially draining for the ranchers. Adding to the cost was the fact that the wolves' presence prevented the cattle from grazing the lush grass west near the mountains. Instead, they spent time in the east, clipping the grass close to the ground. The result was calves weighing one hundred pounds less in the fall. The stress also affected the cows; some aborted, and others didn't breed.

The following summer, it was decided an attempt should be made to radio-collar one of the pack members. That way, we could utilize the collar if they caused future problems. We knew trapping would be tricky due to the large population of grizzly bears in the area. If done right, though, we could minimize the chance of catching one. However, the more bears present, the greater the risk—and this place was crawling with them.

The Fish Wildlife & Parks wolf specialist, Brad, had more time on his hands than I did. He had previously caught and collared wolves there and knew the country, so we decided he would try to accomplish the task. In early summer 2019, Brad camped on one of the nearby ranches, hoping the project wouldn't take long.

Examining pictures from our trail cameras and visiting with other people who used them in the area, we concluded the pack consisted of three or four adults plus an unknown number of pups. For over a month, Brad tried his best. Accomplishing this task was easier said than done. Unlike coyotes, wolves usually stuck together, instead of wandering apart. Pack members were smart and learned from observing others being captured or called in and shot. They seldom forgot.

After a month, Brad called to say that he was pulling out. The adult wolves were wise and difficult to trap. He explained that he would try again later and hopefully capture one of their pups.

The day after Brad left, the rancher phoned me. "Is there *any* chance you can try catching one?" he asked me.

"I can set up some equipment," I replied, "but the time it will take to check day after day is another matter..."

"Two days ago, my grandson, Johnny, spotted three big pups and discovered the wolves' rendezvous site. That narrows the search, right?"

I considered the new developments. "Yeah, that would narrow the search. Okay, yeah. Let's do it." If the wolves hadn't been scared out of there, I had an excellent chance of capturing one.

Of course, I still had to contend with other obstacles. It was mid-summer, meaning the pups were big enough to travel and possibly leave the area. Also, trapping could only be accomplished on a four-wheeler that offered little protection from bears. The rancher gave me directions to where the wolves called home.

No one could ask for a more beautiful workplace than the Rocky Mountain Front, where the Great Plains met the Rockies. Massive mountains stretched north and south. The Blackfeet called them the "Backbone of the World."

To get there, it was eleven miles over a rough two-track trail. I could get closer with a pickup, but the four-wheeler was smoother and four times as fast. The first few miles were rolling grasslands, where, on almost every trip, I saw coyotes, deer, and elk. Halfway to the wolves' location, I paralleled the north side of a deep creek bottom where the cattle grazed. As I passed through, I searched for birds and a possible fresh kill.

The rancher had provided excellent directions. While his grandson had been there on horseback, they had later taken a four-wheeler to pack salt for the cattle. By paying close attention, I could follow the four-wheeler tracks to the location.

The wolves had chosen an excellent area to reside. The steep side of the mountainfront leveled for a short distance and then produced ridges that led downward onto the prairie. My destination was where one of those ridges began and consisted of a flat area perhaps two hundred yards wide and five hundred yards long. Through that flat ran a well-used trail going north and south. The ancient travelway had seen use not only by every animal species that lived in these mountains but also by people who had traveled through there long ago. It was the main route along the mountainfront beneath a towering wall of rock known as the Old North Trail.

While ascending with the four-wheeler, I discovered the path at the mountain's base turned into a steep climb. A rough, steep-sided creek bottom ran to the right. I worried that, if muddy, the trail would be impossible to climb. With the steep mountainside covered in thick stands of aspen and pine to my left, even someone with my experience would have difficulty finding a different route to the trap site on an ATV.

Eventually, the dip at the head of the ridge came into view. It was there they had seen the pups and where I would have my best chance to capture and collar one of the wolves.

It was a narrow pathway through the trees where the trail entered the grassy flat. On my right were thick pines extending upward to a massive rock wall. On my left were pines that covered an upslope for a short distance before the ridge fell downward to the east. Behind me were aspens, willows, pines, and brush alongside the trail I had just climbed. Water springs emerged from the ground.

To me, it looked like bear heaven.

As I eased the four-wheeler through the narrow opening, I spotted wolf tracks on the trail. It was dry now but revealed how often they traveled through there when wet. I entered the grassy park and found a low ridge parallel to the trail on my right covered with pines that ran north and south. Farther ahead and alongside the trail, I passed a small pool where rainwater had collected. Around the pool were large and small wolf tracks. Muddy water in the pad prints revealed the wolves had *just* been there.

Even though my chances were slim, the thought of catching a grizzly bear didn't leave my mind. The Select-A-Catch foot snare I would use had a breakaway connection designed to open and release a larger animal such as a horse, cow, elk, or grizzly. What I worried about the most was the possibility of catching a yearling grizzly or cub. The thought of dealing with an angry sow while sitting on a four-wheeler was not an appealing one.

I drove to the southern end of the grassy park. There, I set two-foot snares ten yards from the trail in a dry creek bottom. It was an excellent place, but there could be a problem with the thick trees on one side if I caught a cub. I turned around, and halfway through the park, a trail revealed wolf tracks that wound through the trees on the low ridge below the rock wall. There, I set one more snare.

On the west side of the trail was a one-way drop into a dark little basin. It was the absolute best location of all. Two paths mingled at the bottom, and wolf scat was everywhere. I had found where they spent their time. If I set there, however, the basin would be surrounded by trees and willows, the worst possible place to deal with a bear.

I decided instead to continue two hundred yards east in the open and set my last two snares in passes that looked like promising travel ways. No urine or scent was used since the wolves had seen those traps before. I knew my best chance to catch one was while it unknowingly walked down the trail.

When finished, I hoped I hadn't scared them away with all the activity.

That evening, I called Andy, our trapper on the Reservation. I told him what was happening and asked if he could accompany me the next day not only to help set up more equipment but also to learn the location in case anything should happen. Andy had been employed with the tribe as a bear technician for six years but now worked for us. When working with bears, there were few people I trusted completely. Andy was one of those who could not only keep it together but was a big powerful man, eager to lend a hand. His great sense of humor lightened any situation.

I met Andy early the next morning. After unloading the four-wheelers, we packed our equipment. Quite a few items needed to be taken: five more foot snares and various trapping equipment such as a hammer, a small shovel, and a screen to filter the dirt over the trap so no rocks or sticks would hamper the snare upon firing. We also brought a looped catch pole to release smaller non-targets and a tranquilizer gun with drugs in case we caught a bigger non-target. We carried pepper spray and a semi-automatic shotgun with slugs for grizzlies.

It was a beautiful morning as we rode the eleven miles to the site, a forty-five-minute drive. Blue skies, sunshine, and no wind.

We stopped two hundred yards before the pass. I uncased my shotgun, a Benelli 12-gauge that held five three-inch slugs, and put one in the chamber. My plan was to have the shotgun in my left hand and rest the butt of the gun on the seat, the barrel pointed upward, ready to use if necessary. Sitting on a four-wheeler provided little protection, and that made me uneasy. I considered the spray but felt the shotgun would be best in such close quarters with an angry bear.

We turned off the four-wheelers and listened. I was relieved not to have any wind. If a cub was caught, it would be vocal, giving us a heads-up.

All was quiet.

We started the four-wheelers and then slowly moved forward. We were tense, alert, and on edge.

We checked the first set.

Nothing.

Then, the next four. All were empty.

Two trail cameras and the mud hole where the fresh tracks had been showed no wolf activity. I had probably scared them away but felt confident they would return. We spent the next few hours setting the five snares we brought and searched for fresh tracks.

The following day, I left home with a mix of emotions. Part of me felt excited about catching a wolf, but I also worried about capturing a bear. Andy would not be joining me. It was one thing to face a situation with others and quite another to do it alone. I loaded my equipment on the four-wheeler I had left locked in an old garage eleven miles from the trap site.

Driving in the first ten miles was routine, but during the last mile, a feeling of apprehension came over me. This project was one of the most dangerous situations I had ever gotten myself into, and the closer I drew to the snares, the scarier it became.

At the bottom of the steep hill going into the site, I turned off the four-wheeler and listened. I then unscabbarded my shotgun and slowly drove forward. It felt much different now, knowing no one was there to help should something suddenly go wrong.

The first set in the open came into view. Nothing.

The second set was hidden in the pines fifteen yards above me and to the right. If something was caught, I would see it or notice the tree was torn up.

I next came up to the sets in the creek bottom on the south end of the grassy park in the pines. Twenty yards away, I saw a broken branch. I got off the four-wheeler and slowly moved forward. The snare loop lay straight on the ground with the breakaway open.

Strands of grizzly hair were snagged on the cable's end.

It had functioned as designed. A large grizzly had been caught, and thankfully, with one pull, the breakaway had opened, allowing the bear to escape.

At the next set, I found a similar situation. However, this time, I could see by the tracks that an elk had been caught and, like the grizzly, had broken free. The snares were reset, and happy to be finished, I drove the four-wheeler off the mountain.

The third morning remained uneventful with nothing captured.

On day four, Andy said he would accompany me. The ranchers' grandson, Johnny, who had initially set up the cameras, also came along.

We stopped the four-wheelers and, after listening for a moment, drove to the first set. They waited while I went forward, cautiously moving toward the second set. The snare was hidden in the trees fifty yards ahead. As I got close, a pine tree began to shake violently, and the unmistakable hiss of a bear could be heard over the idle of the four-wheeler. In a second, my shotgun was raised to my shoulder, and the safety was off without consciously having to think it through.

Staring at the tree, I saw a flash of black through the pine boughs. I sighed in relief—it was just a black bear. At one hundred twenty-five pounds, it was too small to open the breakaway and escape. I turned the four-wheeler around to rejoin my partners. We talked about how crazy that all was and began to prepare a tranquilizer dart.

Sterile water was injected into a small vial containing a powdered drug. After mixing the contents, the appropriate amount, depending on the weight, was extracted with a syringe and transferred to a small aluminum tube. The far end of the cylinder had a rubber stopper containing a small explosive charge. A cap with a short yarn tail screwed into it.

After being filled with the drug, the opposite open side was sealed with another screw cap that had the needle attached. The completed dart was then loaded into the barrel of the dart gun. Behind the dart, a metal device holding a .22-caliber powdered charge was inserted. The barrel was bent closed, and the dart gun was ready to fire. It was quite an experience for Johnny to see how it was done.

Andy and I carefully approached within a distance of twenty feet. I had the shotgun in hand, just in case. Andy's dart found home in the bears' hindquarters. The rest of the operation was smooth and uneventful. After the bear went down, we discovered it was a young male. We transferred him a short distance into the shade to wake up later.

Over the following two days, nothing else was captured. I wanted to get this finished, so I told Andy my idea. The bowl in the thick trees where we had seen all the wolf sign had never left my mind. It was the perfect place to set one more snare and would be our best chance to catch a wolf.

Andy blinked at me like I was crazy. "Do you really want to set a snare in Grizzly Hollow?"

What a name!

But I wasn't deterred.

He knew catching a young grizzly surrounded by thick trees and brush would be a problem. I told him the chances of that happening were slim as our trail cameras hadn't picked up any pictures of sows with cubs. I set the snare while Andy looked on, shaking his head.

The following morning, the snares were empty. It had lightly rained, and we saw tracks of two adult wolves crossing the trail one hundred yards north of our sets. I knew it would just be a matter of time.

On the final morning of our trapping adventure, I was alone. It had been ten days, and not one wolf picture had been taken on the trail cameras, but I never lost hope. I slowly drove the four-wheeler into the trap site with the same anticipation as the days before.

I checked the first five.

Nothing.

To check the snare in Grizzly Hollow, I had to drive up and over a slight ridge on the four-wheeler. Holding the shotgun ready, after topping the ridge, I found a yearling grizzly staring at me from my trap fifteen yards away. My heart raced as I hurriedly put the four-wheeler into reverse, expecting the sow to burst out of the brush at any second.

In all of my years on the job, I had never been in a scarier situation. I should have known better, and I couldn't believe how foolish I had been to set a trap in such a place! There was no way it would turn out well, and I feared the worst was yet to come.

The high point in the mountains was one of the few places on the mountainfront that had cell service. I called Andy and told him the dilemma and how I should have listened to his advice.

"Don't worry, Brother. I'm on my way," he replied. He had a sixty-mile drive, then eleven miles on the four-wheeler, so I knew he would be awhile.

I made a management decision and started pulling equipment; it wasn't worth it. I called the rancher, telling him what had happened and that I was removing my snares. He understood and told me his grandson, Johnny, was there and wanted to drive up and help.

Although Johnny was only seventeen, like a typical ranch kid, he could more than lend a hand. Everything timed out perfectly. I pulled all the sets except the four closest to Grizzly Hollow. I then proceeded to prepare a dart. I had just finished when two four-wheelers popped into view.

Glad to see the guys was an understatement; we visited a minute before I told them we might be lucky. It was a calm day with no wind. I explained that the bear had made no sound all the time I had been there. This was virtually unheard of with captured young grizzlies, especially if the sow was nearby. In a hurry, I hadn't spent much time looking at the bear. It could have been a black bear with a brownish coat. It was possible as some blacks had brown or blond coloration. There was only one way to find out for sure.

I placed the dart gun into the box, and Andy and I drove slowly on the four-wheelers toward the trap site with our shotguns ready. Johnny stayed back to help in any way we might need him. We inched over the low ridge, leaving the ATVs running and in gear.

When the bear came into sight, it looked up at us. Its fur was brown and had blond tips on the top and sides of its shoulders in typical grizzly fashion. Initially, Andy quietly said, "Yeah, it's a grizzly," then, "No, I think it's a black bear." After noticing its narrower head, no hump, and pointed nose, I agreed. What a relief; we might not get killed today after all!

We backed up the four-wheelers and drove a short distance to finish loading the dart. This time, I took the dart gun and Andy the shotgun. The trees made it impossible to dart the bear from the ATV, forcing us to walk in on foot.

How stupid I had been to pick this location.

The bear was positioned in a way that required me to walk around it to get into a darting position. We would have been in serious trouble had it been a young grizzly.

The dart hit its mark, and we moved away. Once sedated, we examined the bear and discovered it was a young male, perhaps three to four years old. It was amazing how much it resembled a cross between a grizzly and a black bear. The bear was lucky in a sense as he would always be safe from being shot by a black bear hunter.

That special place and that day will stay with me forever as it was my last wolf project. Although I helped process several others before retirement, that bear was the final one I captured.

Mike with the grizzly-looking black bear caught with the Select-A-Catch 1000

CONCLUSION

"Forty-two years of work, a lifetime of stories, and a wealth that no amount of money could buy."

Over the course of my career, I saw a pattern—a particular bear, that pair of coyotes, a certain pack of wolves, or that one lion were the ones causing damage. Removing those troublemakers not only saved countless head of livestock but many other innocent predators as well.

Without the help of USDA Wildlife Services, ranchers would be left to their own resources and would have little patience witnessing their livelihood being eaten. The results wouldn't be pretty.

I've always been a strong advocate for non-lethal methods. Guard dogs and electric fences are invaluable tools when they can be implemented. I've always said that if every coyote killed sheep, nobody would be able to have any.

I began my career at twenty years old and retired at sixty-two. Over that time, I came to realize that non-lethal paired with selective removal was—and continues to be—the key. Recently, I told a reporter that if critics of Wildlife Services accompanied me for a week, ninety percent would change their mind about the program, but ten percent never would.

She countered, "If you spent time with bear lovers, you might feel the same way."

"What makes you think I don't like bears?" I asked. "Do you think policemen hate people because of their job?"

She was at a loss for words.

Forty-two years passed in the blink of an eye. How fortunate I was to have a job that I enjoyed going to every day. A job where people were glad to see me when I arrived. A job where I could help balance the struggle between predator and prey. It was truly the best job ever!

Twenty years ago, a friend I was visiting reminded me of an old story. Before my time, a rancher was having coyote problems. While tending his sheep one morning, he spotted a coyote that had just killed a lamb. The rancher grabbed his rifle and shot at the coyote, only to miss and kill an unfortunate sheep standing behind it. Shortly after that, the sheep were sold.

The story came back to me, and I realized I had almost forgotten it. From that day forward, many mornings, I discreetly wrote in a notebook for nearly a year, capturing different stories of my life while they remained fresh in my mind. I did it for my kids, Katie and Chad, so they could understand the life I had lived after I was gone.

No one knew the notebook existed until ten years ago when my wife, Maureen, discovered it. The stories were crude, just the facts. After reading them, she said I needed to write a book. My answer to that was a definitive no. But that was far from the last time Maureen and I discussed the topic. Still, my reply was always the same.

While working in the Sweet Grass Hills one day, a rancher lent me a book titled *Echoes from the Prairie*—it was a history of the people living there. I knew most of the families mentioned in the book, and learning more about their past would be interesting.

As I began to read, it wasn't only the stories of the families I knew but also the history of the families I didn't know that intrigued me. Written in 1976, many of the people featured in the book had lived through the harsh times of the Depression and the Dirty Thirties, and many were homesteaders. It was a fascinating read about how it was and will never be again.

I realized then how many of those people were gone and how fortunate it was that they had recorded their stories before it was too late. When I finished reading, I told Maureen, "It's time to write a book!"

I was fortunate to have lived in a world that no longer exists, a time before cell phones and computers. Back then, we wrote simple weekly reports completed on one sheet of paper. We focused on the job in a world where almost everyone else did the same. I can't imagine a twenty-year-old today living in a remote sheep camp, working off a horse five days a week.

The old trappers, herders, and cowboys I had the fortune of knowing are gone. Pictures of life in those days were rare, and many only remain in my mind. That's one regret—very few pictures. Thankfully, people I worked with through the years shared photos. Many in this book are from them, and for that, I am truly thankful.

Life wasn't always easy, but I don't have a single complaint. Every moment of my life—good or bad, if done over—would not be changed.

Money can never buy happiness or the true love I eventually found. Maureen is my life companion and shared many of the adventures you have just been part of. If not for her, this book would never have been written.

My job didn't pay much, but that never mattered. On the day I retired, I was rich. I had my health, Maureen, and a million dollars worth of memories of when I had been the one between predator and prey.

Mike and his wife, Maureen

ABOUT THE AUTHOR

Mike Hoggan is a retired Wildlife Service Specialist and a part-time sheepherder. He is a passionate historian with an incredible memory for preserving stories before they are forgotten. His love for history and talent for bringing it to life inspired this book—a heartfelt collection of on-the-job memories and experiences that honor the people, places, and events that shaped his life and community.

When not working on the farm alongside his wife Maureen, Mike can usually be found fixing things, putting up hay, or helping the neighbors harvest grain. After years of making things work with only the bare necessities, problem-solving has become second nature to him. His work raising Hampshire and Suffolk sheep brings him both joy and purpose, and he feels truly at home on the farm where he shares hard work, laughter, and quiet moments with Maureen.

For Mike, writing this book was a way to preserve history and the cherished stories he holds close to his heart. It's more than just a recollection; it's a celebration of the people, lessons, values, and animals that give meaning to our lives. Mike and Maureen live in the untamed beauty of Montana.

www.ingramcontent.com/pod-product-compliance
Lightning Source LLC
Chambersburg PA
CBHW052028030426
42337CB00027B/4913